POLITICAL PROFILES

OF

BLACK

COLLEGE STUDENTS

IN

THE SOUTH

Socio-political Attitudes, Preferences,
Personality and Characteristics

J. Dudley McClain, Jr.
West Georgia College
University System of Georgia

SOUTHERN COLLEGE STUDENT PROFILES

Resurgens Publications, Inc.

Atlanta

POLITICAL PROFILES OF
BLACK COLLEGE STUDENTS IN THE SOUTH:

Socio-political Attitudes, Preferences, Personality and Characteristics

ISBN 0-89583-002-7
Library of Congress Catalogue Card Number: 77-82709

Manufactured in the United States of America.

 Resurgens Publications, Inc.

Atlanta, Georgia, U.S.A.

The several volumes of these

SOUTHERN COLLEGE STUDENT PROFILES

are dedicated to

my parents

and to

Dehryl, Debra, Dawn and Mike

and to

the millions of Americans in the
South, black and white, who have
made their way through the most
profound social and political
change in our national history
with a degree of success that
has made the South a worthy
example for the remainder of the
nation and the rest of the world.

PREFACE

This book of data profiles on black students in colleges and universities in the South is one of a number in the author's Southern College Student Profiles series. Other volumes of socio-political profiles which will be included in the series are those dealing with: College Students in the South; White College Students in the South; College Students in Southern Appalachia; and Female College Students in the South. The same data format and system of numbering of tables is followed in each volume in the series to facilitate ready comparison of all data for each separate group studied.

The data on which the several volumes in the series are based were derived from the responses of 11,282 students who were interviewed in four separate groups of interviews at fifty colleges and universities in the eleven states of the old Confederacy during the period from late Spring, 1972, through early Fall, 1973. Two groups of interviews were completed prior to the 1972 election and the revelation of the Watergate scandals, and the other two groups of interviews were completed following those events.

The study touches a wide range of topics, including students' political participation and orientation, politically supportive attitudes, personality variables, feelings toward various political interest groups and political figures, preferences for the presidency, attitudes on labor policy questions, and background characteristics.

The study breaks new ground in the field of political socialization and constitutes a significant addition to the literature, in that it presents the first in-depth consideration of the political attitudes and preferences of this most significant group of new, young voters in the most atypical region of the nation. Together, the volumes in the series thus comprise a definitive study and offer valuable insights into the political mind of this significant group, one from which will come many of the future leaders of this rapidly changing and unique part of America.

v

ACKNOWLEDGEMENTS

I **wish** to express my appreciation for the financial support afforded this project by West Georgia College and to acknowledge the influence and assistance of the numerous friends, colleagues and students who contributed in various ways and at various stages to the study upon which this report is based.

Gordon Henderson and Raymond Wells were most responible for my initial interest in survey research and in the relationship between political attitudes and support for the political system in democracies. My interest in teaching was initially stimulated and often reinforced over many years by my mentor and friend, Lynwood Holland. My contacts with numerous students at Texas Tech University and West Georgia College and the other institutions at which I have taught have provided constant and continuous rejuvenation of these interests.

I owe a great debt to the more than three hundred colleagues who administered the survey questionnaire at the fifty schools at which my study was conducted and to the more than eleven thousand college and university students who participated. I am particularly indebted to the faculty member at each school who gave so generously of his or her time and energies in coordinating the project at each institution. They included: Moses Akpan, Walton Bagley, Chester Bain, Rick Barrett, David Bass, Thomas Bellows, Edwin Coulter, C. B. Crabb, James Dennis, Don Fairchild, C. N. Fortenberry, Jerry Gilbert, David Grubbs, John Hamilton, Samuel Hamlett, Robert Harris, William Hatcher, J. F. Herndon, Lois Hollis, Ellerd Hulbert, Gilford Jackson, Shelly Jarmon, Mel Jones, David Jordan, S. J. Kim, Earl Kline, Robert McChesney, Leslie McLemore, Fred March, Penelope Maza, Al Melton, D. R. Moberg, Charles Mobley, Bill Morrow, William Nelson, Salvatore Nerboso, Edgar Nesman, Patrick O'Connor, Maurice O'Donnell, Beryl Pettus, Ferinez Phelps, Tom Phillips, Sydney Reed, E. F. Russell, Steven Sanderson, Charles Sherman, Yawsoon Sim, Mac Simpson, Amarjite Singh, Frank Smith, Jerry Smith, Paul Stephenson, Bob Toburen, William Troutman, Jack Turner,

Thomas Ungs, Tom Vandervort, Donald Vaughan, Kenneth Walker, Earl Wallace, Ed Westen, Raymond Wheeler, Nelson Wikstrom, and William Young.

The reduction of 11,282 students' responses for the 227 variable items derived from the eighteen-page questionnaire used in the study proved a prodigious task. I am deeply indebted to students Marcella Bolden, Lynn Dooley, Tom Maley and, especially, Elaine Trimm, and to members of the West Georgia College Computer Center staff for their assistance with this aspect of the project. Eloise Perry, Larry Hitch and Toni Medlin, of the computer center staff, have rendered invaluable assistance in establishing the necessary data files and obtaining various data analyses for me. Richard Slaughter has offered valuable suggestions with regard to my presentation of data. Roland Smith has given most generously of his time and energies in assisting me with computer programs available at Texas Tech University, but not available to me at my own school.

Jessica Lee typed the questionnaire drafts through my several revisions of the survey instrument. Jimmy Drew and James Harrington were of great help in printing them. Sue Myers has performed yeoman service in the typing of this manuscript, with its numerous tables, and throughout the ordeal has maintained her usual good humor and tolerance; I am most appreciative. I am indebted to Dean Richard Dangle for her services. Sandy Butler and Dawn McClain endured with me the proofreading of the many tables which have been included.

There is no adequate way to acknowledge the aid and comfort afforded me by those whose support meant the most to me throughout the more than five years over which this study has extended—my wife Dehryl, and my three children, Debra, Dawn and Mike. They have shown unfailing patience and understanding while a husband and father devoted entirely too much of his time and energies to this project. They can never really know how much this has meant to me during these labors. It is to them, most of all, that I am indebted.

CONTENTS

I
SOUTHERN COLLEGE STUDENT SURVEY PROJECT

INTRODUCTION

College students in general have in recent years been highly vocal critics of the American political system, many of the traditional values of our society, public officials, and their parents' generation of voters. Black college students in the South have frequently been in the vanguard of both civil rights and student protest movements. Until ratification of the Twenty-Sixth Amendment, most college students in this country were denied the right to vote through age limitations established by the various states. In addition, blacks in the South were until only recently effectively denied the right to vote across the South. They were thus denied one of the more obvious means through which they might have sought to bring about fundamental changes in the politics of the nation and in the society they so vehemently and consistently criticized. The civil rights movement and various legislative enactments and programs have in the last few years, however, extended the suffrage in a meaningful way to blacks in the South. In 1972 college students, including black students, had the vote in every state for the first time in a presidential election. Their addition to the American electorate raises a number of obvious questions about their impact upon American politics. The impact of the black college student voter upon the politics of the South is of particular moment.

What was the impact, if any, of this group of new minority-group voters in the first presidential campaign year during which they were enfranchised? What are the implications for the traditional voting patterns of voting behavior in this country of their addition to the voting rolls of each of the eleven states of the South? Are these new black student voters significantly "different" in their political attitudes and preferences from their parents, or are they merely "mirrors" of their parents, as many of the studies in the literature of political socialization suggest? Do they reflect attitudes and preferences

3

similar to those of other major groups of voters, or
are their politics in conflict with those of other
major political interest groups? In the American South,
are they as far removed from the "mainstream" of
American politics as the white voters of the region
traditionally have been? What conclusions, if any,
may we draw from their expressed attitudes and
preferences with regard to the likely course of the
politics of this region relative to the politics of
the nation as a whole? This book provides for the
first time considerable insight into these and other
questions about this important group of new black
voters.

This is a book which presents a wide range of new
information about the political attitudes and preferences of almost two thousand black college and
university students in 12 of the public colleges and
universities in the 11 states of the American South
which have traditionally had essentially black, or
"minority" student bodies. The purpose of this book
is to make available a very substantial amount of
original data about the politics of this one important
racial subgroup within the youngest age cohort within
the larger group of new voters in the country. The
new data this book presents were obtained during the
course of and immediately following the first
presidential election year during which eighteen-year-
olds were eligible to vote across the entire nation.
This new information about this new group of black
voters is of particular interest at this time, as we
reflect upon the two elections in which they have
been eligible to vote in presidential caucuses and
primaries and in the national election.

This report on black college student politics in
the South, on their political attitudes and preferences,
is thus neither conceptual nor theoretical in its
approach. The book constitutes a straightforward
report which is purposely descriptive in format. It
does, however, constitute an in-depth study of the
political attitudes and preferences of this important
group of new black voters in a politically atypical
region of the country in the unusually turbulent
"Watergate" era of American history.

The decades of the 1950's and 1960's saw a great deal of unrest and disruption of the American political process by black college students. The civil rights movement, the various campus riots, and the many aspects of the political controversy rising out of America's involvement in Viet Nam all served as focal points of black student unrest, alienation, and distrust of political leadership. These were followed by the traumatic and particularly frustrating disclosures of the Watergate period, which we may reasonably surmise would have resulted in even lower levels of support among blacks than among whites for the political system and for persons in positions of public trust.

Yet black college students, like college students in general, today seem either to have turned to the more pragmatic considerations of preparing to earn a living or to an even more apathetic, negativistic, even fatalistic view of their likely impact upon the American political process. The black college student of the 1970's, like his or her white counterpart, presents the outward appearance of one quite different from his or her predecessor of the last decade. The several volumes in this series are not concerned with the cause of such change, if indeed there has been any such fundamental change in the black college student in this region. They are concerned instead with the presentation of much new information about this group. They describe; they do not attempt to explain. Yet what they tell us about the black college student in the South has not previously been available to us.

Just what sort of political being is the black college student in the South in the 1970's? Are the black college students of this decade supportive of system values and democratic political processes? Or have they simply "given up" on our political system and our political leadership and concluded that they cannot bring about any meaningful changes? Are they trustful of public officials? Are they politically efficacious? Are they politically alienated? In their personal perspectives, are they conservative?

Are they cynical? Do they reflect an authoritarian
point of view? Which interest groups do they favor,
and which do they view with disfavor? Which national
political figures do they like? Which ones do they not
like? Are blacks and whites among college students in
this region alike in these respects, or do they reflect
attitudes and preferences which are fundamentally
different? Did black college students who were interviewed prior to the 1972 election and the revelations
of the Watergate scandals reflect attitudes and preferences which were essentially different from those
expressed by black students interviewed after broad
exposure of those matters? With which interest groups
do they identify? Which do they dislike? And which
public figures and presidential candidates did they
favor during this period? Would there have been any
changes in their choices for the presidency had George
Wallace been in the race as an independent or third-
party candidate? What were their choices without a
Wallace third-party candidacy?

This book provides new insights into the views of
black college students in the South on these and other
points. The other volumes in this series present
similar information about still other subgroups among
southern college students. No argument is made that
the black students who were interviewed constituted a
"random" sample; thus, no argument is advanced that
the results constitute "proof" of anything about the
black college student voter in the South. No argument
is made that the results have statistical significance.
These data are valuable in that they do tell us much
about these new black voters. They may suggest something of the impact of this group, from which will come
many of the black leaders of the region in the years
ahead, upon the politics of the region. For these and
still other reasons, the data are worth our consideration. The reader is, for the moment, left to draw his
or her own conclusions about the importance and mean-
ings of these findings. The conclusions of the author
will be presented in his forthcoming book on the political socialization of college students in the South.

THE BLACK SOUTHERN COLLEGE STUDENT STUDY

A number of the most fundamental assumptions about our political system have been challenged in recent years. This was especially the case during the Viet Nam and Watergate eras. Seldom, if ever, in our entire national history have these long-standing basic assumptions about the role of the average citizen in a democracy been subject to more constant or more serious challenge than during and since those traumatic national experiences. The viability of our political system has been questioned more seriously on very few other occasions. The failure of public officials to live up to the trust placed in them by the electorate has discouraged and frustrated many Americans; perhaps no group has been more dismayed and frustrated than have blacks by the misconduct and inequities revealed during the Viet Nam and Watergate episodes.

This study of new, young black voters in the South has obvious implications for the field of political socialization. The data presented in this book have more immediate implications which stem from these traumatic national experiences, particularly those of Watergate, which may have caused substantial rises in the levels of mistrust, inefficacy, alienation, personal conservatism, authoritarianism, cynicism, political obligation or law-abidingness, and political participation among the young college-student voters entering the political life of a democratic nation and which may thereby have influenced their perceptions of their own role as participants in the democratic political process.

To the extent dysfunctional attitudes may have been heightened by the events of Watergate and Viet Nam, the increase may have been even greater among blacks than among whites. This study presents the first detailed picture of the political attitudes of black college students in the South and of their feelings toward a wide variety of interest groups and feelings. It is the first look at their attitudes of support for the democratic political system in this nation.

7

Access to the political process through the vote became a reality for those from eighteen to twenty-one years of age through the three-step process which began with (1) passage by Congress in 1970 of the 1970 Voting Rights Act,[1] continued with (2) the decision of the United States Supreme Court in U.S. v. Arizona[2] that the law was unconstitutional, and culminated in (3) the subsequent proposal by Congress and ratification by the states by June 30, 1970, of the Twenty-Sixth Amendment,[3] establishing the right to vote in federal as well as state elections at age eighteen.

The potential impact of the eighteen-to-twenty-one-year-old vote upon our electoral process is evidenced by Census Bureau estimates that in the 1972 presidential election there were more than 25 million more people eligible to vote than had been eligible in 1968. More than 11 million young people had the vote in the 1972 election than had been the case in 1968. Of these 11 million newly enfranchised voters, the Census Bureau estimated that 4 million were college students.[4] Nearly one of every two new voters in 1972 was in the eighteen through twenty age group. Approximately one of every six new voters in 1972 was a college student.[5]

In assessing the potential of the new, young black voter in the politics of the South, we must note the vastly increased significance of the black vote in general in this region. Sixty-four of the ninety Congressional districts across the nation which had the highest percent of black population were in the South, according to the 1960 Census figures. It has been estimated that the number of registered Negro voters in the South increased by some 938,000 in the eleven states covered by this study between the 1964 and 1968 elections.[6] Although perhaps a smaller proportion of blacks in the South attend college than is the case in other regions of the country, blacks comprise a higher proportion of the electorate in the South than elsewhere. Many of the future political leaders among blacks in the South and the nation will come from those blacks now enrolled in colleges in the South. A number of the black students who were interviewed in this study will no doubt become prominant political figures in their own right in the years ahead.

It may also be appropriate to note the dramatic
increase in voter turnout in general in the South, as
contrasted with the rest of the nation, in appraising
the potential impact of the new, young college student
voter upon the politics of this traditionally conservative region.   The percentage of the total national voter
turnout coming from these eleven Southern states increased from 14.9 percent in 1960 to 21.2 by 1968.   The
total number of votes cast across the nation in 1968
was 73,211,562; of those, 14,803,725 came from these
eleven Southern states.   The national total increased by
only 4,373,343 altogether; that of these eleven Southern
states increased by a larger number, by 4,531,835.[7]   The
viability of the candidacy for the presidency in 1976
of a former governor of a Deep South state has proven
to be the first such viable candidacy since before the
Civil War.   The fact that numerous respected black
political leaders and rank-and-file black voters in the
South were among his most significant and early support-
ers gives ample evidence of a new day in the politics
of the South, one in which blacks have moved effectively
into the mainstream of the political life of the region.

In the wake of various riots by blacks during the
decade of the 1960's, it became all too commonplace a
practice on the part of many in this country, and particularly in the South, to blame blacks, and particularly to blame black college students, for the apparent
instability of the American political process.   Yet the
critics of the black college student seldom cited con-
crete data or other evidence in support of their criti-
cisms.   They consistently attributed the attitudes and
behavior of a relatively small number of black activists
to black college students in general.

Today, few would debate seriously the importance of
the millions of new college-student voters and that of
the hundreds of thousands of new black college-student
voters to our political system or their potential impact
upon the future politics of the nation and the South.
It is obviously highly important to our democratic form
of government what these students, with their potential
and prospects for meaningful political participation and
leadership in the decades to come, think and feel about
their opportunities and capacity for meaningful

participation in the political process. It is highly important that we know something of their attitudes toward that process and that system, whether they hold politically supportive or disruptive attitudes, as we consider their impact upon American politics.

It is important, too, to the political life of the South and the nation to know something of the orientation of the young black voter in the South, a region heretofore characterized by the one-party, non-competitive politics of racism and extreme conservatism. It is likely that any change that may be in the offing in the politics of the South will be reflected in some measure by the political attitudes and preferences, the orientation toward parties, candidates and issues, and the degree of support for the democratic political process shown by the millions of new young voters in the region. Black voters may well hold the balance of political power in the South in the years to come. Black political leadership in the South may well be found in those years to have come from today's black college student population in the South. Today's black college student in the South will no doubt have much to say about the character and nature of any "New South" of the future.

If effective political participation, or at least the feeling of effective political participation, is essential to the viability and survivability of a democratic political system, then it is indeed imperative to consider both the extent and the nature of participation in that process, as well as the attitudes that may shape the quality of the participation. The attitudes and participation of newcomers to that process are especially important. Their study becomes even more vital in those rare instances in which unusually large numbers of new participants of an entirely different subgroup, such as college student voters, or such as previously disenfranchised minority-group voters, enter the political life of a region of the nation for the first time.

Politically significant attitudes may themselves appropriately be considered in light of the social and cultural environment in which a new subgroup has formulated those attitudes. This is particularly true in the case of a previously-disenfranchised group such as blacks in the South, a region which has throughout most of our nation's history been out of the mainstream of American politics and thus atypical of American politics. It may be even more significant to consider the attitudes of such a new subgroup when it is found within a region which has distinctive and "parochial" regional subculture.

The literature of political socialization strongly suggests the existence of a relationship between political attitudes and participation in the political process. Few studies to date have undertaken to measure the direct impact of historical events, such as the Watergate scandals upon either the levels and kinds of political participation or the attitudes that may affect that participation. If it is correct to hypothesize that distrustful citizens constitute a barrier to the success of the political system, then the implications of distrust of public officials and government are obvious.

The survey project upon which this book is based was first directed toward the impact upon the political process of the college-student voters added to our voting rolls by the Twenty-Sixth Amendment. Following the general exposure of the Watergate scandals, however, it became obvious that such a study should also cover attitudes in the post-Watergate, post-election period. The project was thus extended to obtain similar measurements following the 1972 election. Since there had initially been no expectation of extending the study beyond the election, it was not possible to interview the same students a second time following the election; there was no way of knowing the names of those interviewed in the months preceding the election.

The study was thus not a panel study; it did not involve interviews of the same students following the election who had been interviewed prior to it. One might assume, however, that revelations about the Watergate events might have had some impact upon the attitudes of college students in general and black college students in particular by the time of the post-election interviews. James McCord's letter of March 23, 1973, threatening to reveal matters of which he had knowledge, and President Nixon's television address to the nation on April 30, 1973, are likely indicators that the public had by then become aware of Watergate.

Were there any discernible differences in the overall response patterns of black college students in the South from the time of the "pre-Watergate," pre-election interviews to the time of the "post-Watergate," post-election interviews? If so, could these differences reasonably be assumed to be in some measure the product of the exposure of the students to the controversy of Watergate? We can only speculate. The data presented in this book are intended to facilitate and perhaps heighten that speculation.

Survey and Questionnaire

The content of the questionnaire had already been determined prior to the time the focus of the study was broadened following disclosure of the Watergate scandals. Only slight modifications of the questionnaire were required, however, to fit its contents to the "post-Watergate" situation.

A decision was reached to obtain a number of interviews sufficiently large to be considered "representative," though not "random" in the usual sense. This largely determined the other aspects of research design. The level of conceptualization was in most respects classificatory; it was to a limited degree comparative. Had the samples been "random," the level of conceptualization would have allowed the use of nominal and ordinal levels of measurement. Only nominal level tests would in any event have been appropriate for the great majority of the attributes and variables sampled; ordinal level tests would have been appropriate for the various attitudinal indices that were contemplated, but for very few of the remaining variables. The decision to use a stratified, non-random group of interviews dictated that presentation and analysis of the data would be essentially descriptive, relying primarily upon inference and upon induction from the data.

An eighteen-page pre-coded, closed-ended, self-administered survey instrument was designed to obtain responses to more than two hundred items. The questionnaire was completed by students in introductory level social science classes; it was administered in the main to students in introductory level classes in political science and American government.

The questionnaire included a number of items from the literature of political science, political socialization, and political psychology, which have been used and reported by others in a number of prior studies. The questions included measures of political efficacy, trust in government, alienation, authoritarianism, personal cynicism or personal effectiveness, personal conservatism, civic obligation or law-abidingness, and partisan identification. Also included were other items designed to obtain socio-demographic data, such as age, marital status, level of educational aspiration, years of college completed, expected college major, intended occupational field, status as a veteran or non-veteran, family union ties, religious preference, frequency of church attendance, socioeconomic self-perception, racial or ethnic background, perception of family income level, level of education of parents, employment status of head of household, and occupation of head of household.[9]

The first two groups of interviews were conducted during the Spring and Fall months, respectively, of 1972. Of those interviewed prior to the election only Group II is reported upon here, since the only other minority school (Albany State College) was in Group I and no "minority" schools were in Group IV. All of the responses in the first of these two groups reported here were thus obtained prior to the Presidential election of 1972 and prior to the time the public became widely aware of the seriousness of the Watergate questions.

The interviews comprising the third group were completed during the Spring of 1973 and were thus all obtained after the election and after the public had in all likelihood become generally aware of the implications of Watergate.

In Group I, a total of 2,812 students at 11 institutions in the 4 states of Alabama, Florida, Georgia and

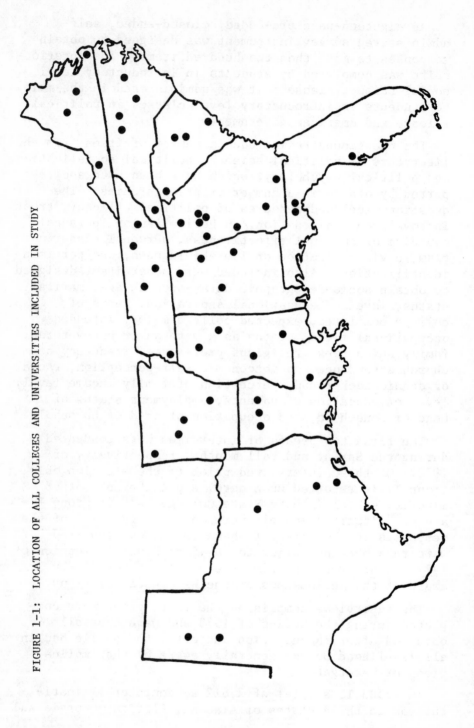

FIGURE 1-1: LOCATION OF ALL COLLEGES AND UNIVERSITIES INCLUDED IN STUDY

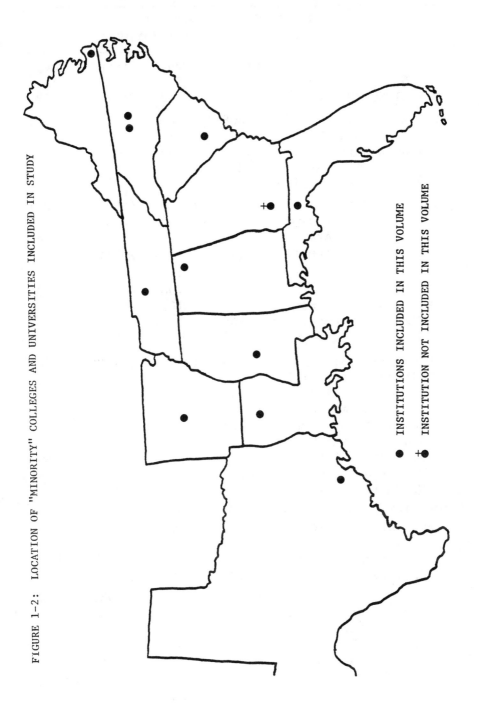

FIGURE 1-2: LOCATION OF "MINORITY" COLLEGES AND UNIVERSITIES INCLUDED IN STUDY

● INSTITUTIONS INCLUDED IN THIS VOLUME

+ INSTITUTION NOT INCLUDED IN THIS VOLUME

TABLE 1-1: NUMBER AND TIME OF INTERVIEWS—
ALL STUDENTS AT ALL INSTITUTIONS.

STATE & INSTITUTION	Group I Sp 72	Group II F 72	Group III Sp 73	Group IV F 73
ALABAMA (914)	(408)	(506)	(0)	(0)
*Ala. A. & M. Univ.		213		
Auburn University		293		
Jacksonville St. U.	267			
Univ. of Montevallo	141			
ARKANSAS (825)	(0)	(0)	(617)	(208)
Ark. Poly. College			138	
St. Col. of Ark.				208
U./Ark. Fayetteville			375	
*U./Ark. Pine Bluff			104	
FLORIDA (558)	(264)	(108)	(186)	(0)
*Fla. A. & M. Univ.		108		
Fla. State Univ.	264			
U. of So. Fla.			186	
GEORGIA (1,659)	(1028)	(0)	(345)	(286)
*Albany State Col.	172			
Columbus College	231			
DeKalb Comm. College				146
Ga. Inst. of Tech.	220			
Georgia State Univ.	212			
N. Georgia College				140
Valdosta St. Col.	193			
W. Georgia College			345	
LOUISIANA (931)	(0)	(931)	(0)	(0)
*Grambling College		204		
Louisiana State U.		208		
Louisiana Tech. U.		232		
Northeast La. St. U.		287		
MISSISSIPPI (952)	(0)	(794)	(158)	(0)
*Jackson State Col.		167		
Miss. State Univ.		248		
Univ. of Miss.		379		
Univ. of So. Miss.			158	

TABLE 1-1:   NUMBER AND TIME OF INTERVIEWS–
ALL STUDENTS AT ALL INSTITUTIONS.

STATE & INSTITUTION	GROUP I Sp 72	GROUP II F 72	GROUP III Sp 73	GROUP IV F 73
NORTH CAROLINA (936)	(0)	(0)	(638)	(298)
E. Carolina Univ.			335	
*N. C. A. & T. U.			82	
*N. C. Central U.			81	
U. of N. Carolina				298
W. Carolina Univ.			140	
SOUTH CAROLINA (986)	(0)	(598)	(388)	(0)
Clemson University		273		
Col. of Charleston			161	
*S. C. State College			227	
U. of S. Carolina		325		
TENNESSEE (1,089)	(0)	(989)	(0)	(100)
Memphis State Univ.		204		
Middle Tenn. St. U.		218		
*Tenn. State Univ.		183		
Tenn. Tech. Univ.				100
Univ. of Tennessee		384		
TEXAS (1,753)	(1112)	(0)	(641)	(0)
Sam Houston State U.	403			
*Texas Southern U.			354	
Texas Tech Univ.	316			
U./Tex. Arlington			287	
W. Texas State U.	393			
VIRGINIA (679)	(0)	(0)	(561)	(118)
*Norfolk State Univ.			142	
Univ. of Virginia			165	
Va. Commonwealth U.				118
Va. Polytech. Inst.			254	
TOTALS (11,282)	(2812)	(3926)	(3534)	(1010)
MINORITY SCHOOLS (2037)	(172)	(875)	(990)	(0)
OTHER SCHOOLS (9245)	(2640)	(3051)	(2544)	(1010)

TABLE 1-2:   NUMBER AND TIME OF INTERVIEW-
BLACK STUDENTS AT ALL INSTITUTIONS.

STATE & INSTITUTION	Group I Sp 72	Group II F 72	Group III Sp 73	Group IV F 73
ALABAMA (200)	(10)	(190)	(0)	(0)
*Ala. A. & M. U.		188		
Auburn U.		2		
Jacksonville St.	8			
U. of Montevallo	2			
ARKANSAS (111)	(0)	(0)	(103)	(8)
Ark. Poly. College			1	
St. Col. of Ark.				8
U. of Arkansas			13	
*Ark. at Pine Bluff			89	
FLORIDA (127)	(32)	(90)	(5)	(0)
*Fla. A. & M. U.		90		
Florida State U.	32			
U. of S. Florida			5	
GEORGIA (243)	(208)	(0)	(22)	(13)
Albany State Col.	151			
Columbus College	16			
DeKalb Comm. College				11
Ga. Inst. of Tech.	1			
Georgia State U.	32			
N. Georgia College				2
Valdosta St. Col.	8			
W. Georgia College			22	
LOUISIANA (227)	(0)	(227)	(0)	(0)
*Grambling College		197		
Louisiana State U.		1		
Louisiana Tech U.		8		
Northeast La. St.		21		
MISSISSIPPI (175)	(0)	(165)	(10)	(0)
*Jackson State Col.		157		
Miss. State U.		3		
U. of Mississippi		5		
U. of S. Miss.			10	

TABLE 1-2: NUMBER AND TIME OF INTERVIEW-
BLACK STUDENTS AT ALL INSTITUTIONS.

STATE & INSTITUTIONS	Group I Sp 72	Group II F 72	Group III Sp 73	Group IV F 73
NORTH CAROLINA (172)	(0)	(0)	(160)	(12)
E. Carolina U.			11	
*N. C. A. & T. U.			78	
*N. C. Central U.			69	
U. of N. Carolina				12
W. Carolina Univ.			2	
SOUTH CAROLINA (242)	(0)	(22)	(220)	(0)
Clemson U.		4		
Col. of Charleston			15	
*S. C. State Col.			205	
U. of S. Carolina		18		
TENNESSEE (222)	(0)	(220)	(0)	(2)
Memphis State U.		26		
Middle Tenn. St.		10		
*Tenn. State U.		168		
Tenn. Tech. U.				2
U. of Tennessee		16		
TEXAS (349)	(32)	(0)	(317)	(0)
Sam Houston State	17			
*Texas Southern U.			309	
Texas Tech U.	8			
U.T./Arlington			8	
W. Texas State U.	7			
VIRGINIA (163)	(0)	(0)	(147)	(16)
*Norfolk State U.			136	
U. of Virginia			8	
Va. Commonwealth U.				16
Va. Polytechnic U.			3	
AT ALL SCHOOLS (2,231)	(282)	(*914)	(*984)	(51)

*Reported in this volume

TABLE 1-3: NUMBERS AND TIME OF INTERVIEWS-
            ALL STUDENTS AT MINORITY INSTITUTIONS.

STATE & INSTITUTIONS	Group I Sp 72	Group II F 72	Group III Sp 73	Group IV F 73
ALABAMA				
Ala. A. & M. Univ.		213		
ARKANSAS				
U./Ark. Pine Bluff			104	
FLORIDA				
Fla. A. & M. Univ.		108		
GEORGIA				
Albany State Col.	172			
LOUISIANA				
Grambling College		204		
MISSISSIPPI				
Jackson State Col.		167		
NORTH CAROLINA				
N. C. A. & T. U.			82	
N. C. Central U.			81	
SOUTH CAROLINA				
S. C. State College			227	
TENNESSEE				
Tenn. State Univ.		183		
TEXAS				
Texas Southern U.			354	
VIRGINIA				
Norfolk State Univ.			142	
TOTAL NO. OF STUDENTS	172	875	990	0

TABLE 1-4: NUMBER AND TIME OF INTERVIEWS-
BLACK STUDENTS AT MINORITY INSTITUTIONS.

STATE & INSTITUTION	Group I Sp 72	Group II F 72	Group III Sp 73	Group IV F 73
ALABAMA				
Ala. A. & M. U.		188		
ARKANSAS				
U./Ark. Pine Bluff			89	
FLORIDA				
Fla. A. & M. Univ.		90		
GEORGIA				
Albany State Col.	151			
LOUISIANA				
Grambling College		197		
MISSISSIPPI				
Jackson State Col.		157		
NORTH CAROLINA				
N. C. A. & T. U.			78	
N. C. Central U.			69	
SOUTH CAROLINA				
S. C. State Col.			205	
TENNESSEE				
Tenn. State U.		168		
TEXAS				
Texas Southern U.			309	
VIRGINIA				
Norfolk State U.			136	
TOTAL NO. OF BLACKS	151	800	886	0

Texas completed the survey instrument. Of these, only
172 were enrolled in a "minority" or predominantly
"black" school. All of these were at a single school
in Georgia. They have not been included in this report.
In Group II, a total of 3,926 at 10 schools in the 6
states of Alabama, Florida, Louisiana, Mississippi,
South Carolina and Tennessee completed the questionnaire.
Of these, 875 were students at 5 minority schools. A
total of 914 indicated that they were "Black-American."
They comprise "Group II" as reported in this volume.

After the decision to expand the study because of the
implications of the Watergate matter, two additional
groups of students were interviewed at comparable times
of the next year at still other colleges and universities in the Southern states. This was done in order
to facilitate a comparison of the pre-election, pre-
Watergate period, following Nixon's landslide victory
and the subsequent revelations of the magnitude of the
Watergate scandals.

Group III included 3,535 students from 17 schools in
the 8 states of Arkansas, Florida, Georgia, Mississippi,
North Carolina, South Carolina, Texas and Virginia. The
study was conducted at these schools in April and May,
1973, with the sole exception of one school at which the
study was completed near the middle of March. Group III
included 990 responses from students at 6 minority
schools in the 5 states of Arkansas, North Carolina,
South Carolina, Texas and Virginia. A total of 984 of
those in Group III indicated that they were "Black-
American." They make up "Group III" as reported in this
volume. None of the students included in Group IV were
at minority schools. Only a very few were black. Blacks
in Group IV have therefore not been included in this
volume.

Background Characteristics of Black Students Interviewed

As one would expect in the case of responses from
public colleges and universities, the vast majority
(93%) of the black students, as was the case with other
groups, gave as their state of residence one of the
Southern states in which the study was conducted. The

percentages of black students who listed each of the 11 states as their permanent residence were: Alabama (9.5%); Arkansas (4.8%); Florida (6.2%); Georgia (10.3%); Louisiana (9.7%); Mississippi (7.6%); North Carolina (6.9%); South Carolina (9.8%); Tennessee (7.7%); Texas (13.8%); and Virginia (7.0%). With the sole exception of Illinois (1.1%), no state other than one of these 11 Southern states was listed as the state of residence of as much as 1% of the black students responding.

Males comprised 42% of the black students interviewed, females 56%, with 2% not indicating their sex.

"Black-Americans" comprised 19.8% of the 11,282 students interviewed. As would also be anticipated, the vast majority (90%) of the black students interviewed were between eighteen and twenty-five years of age. Those under thirty constituted 94% of the sample; less than 4% were over thirty years old. Just over 2% failed to indicate their ages.

Slightly more than 71% of the blacks interviewed expressed a preference for one of the Protestant denominations, while almost 6.5% said they preferred Catholicism, only .4% indicated they preferred Judiasm, 14% expressed some other denominational preference, 3% said they preferred none of the organized churches, 2% claimed to be agnostics, and 1% claimed to be atheists.

The students were also asked what they believed their families' annual incomes were. The black students answers showed that 30.2% believed it to be less than $6,999, that 20.1% thought it would range between $6,000 and $9,999, that 14.8% believed it would fall between $10,000 and $14,999, that 8.7% felt it would be between $15,000 and $24,999 per year, and that only 3% thought it was more than $25,000 per annum.

Those interviewed were also asked to identify the socioeconomic class within which they thought their families would best be described as fitting. Of the blacks, only 4.7% said "upper" class, and just 1.3% said "lower" class. Almost one-fourth (24.1%) said "upper-middle" class, whereas 36.6% said "working" class. Approximately one-fourth, or 24,3% said "middle-middle" class.

II
SURVEY QUESTIONNAIRE
AND DATA CODING OUTLINE

SURVEY QUESTIONNAIRE AND DATA CODING OUTLINE

The coding scheme used for most of the data derived
from the survey questionnaire which was administered in
the 1972-1973 Southern College Student Study is indicated on the face of the questionnaire. For each question,
the numbers within the question item itself show the
values assigned the responses in coding the answers.
For the questions using the "feeling thermometer"
(questions 4, 5, and 6 on pages 6 and 7), the values
assigned the responses in coding the answers are shown
at the left margin beside the thermometer "degree" levels
on the unnumbered page in the questionnaire which
explains the use of the thermometer device. The only
variation from the coding scheme which is shown in this
section involved the coding of "non-responses" and
"refusals" as "0" values in the appropriate columns for
students from whom no responses were obtained.

The pages of this section which follow the part which
is comprised of the survey questionnaire continue the
delineation of the coding scheme used for additional
data which were derived: from listing of the institutions at which the students participating in the study
were enrolled; from recoding of certain variables from
other column locations; and from computation of a number
of "four-level" and "two-level" index scores, "relative"
and "absolute," based upon the responses to the several
series of question items in the survey instrument.

Index scores have been created for each of the series
of questions measuring three politically-supportive
attitudes (political trust, political efficacy, and
political obligation or law-abidingness) and four
personality variables (personal conservatism, personal
authoritarianism, personal cynicism, and personal alienation). Question items in each series which failed to
correlate positively with other items in the series were
not used in constructing the indices.

Four different indices have been constructed for each
of these seven question series: (1) a four-level "relative" index, based upon an arbitrary, researcher-effected
response distribution which yielded the most nearly "even"

27

frequency distribution which was possible and which in
each case measured four different "levels" of the
responses to the variable series; (2) a two-level "relative" index, also yielding the most "even" possible
frequency distribution, but reflecting only whether the
responses "did" or "did not" reflect the attitude or
trait being measured; (3) a four-level "absolute" index,
based upon the "actual" or "chance" frequency distribution which resulted from a simple division into index-
score ranges on the basis of the response values
assigned to each responses (without any attempt being
made to effect any arbitrary "even" frequency distribution, as was done with the four-level "relative" index
scores); and (4) a two-level "absolute" index also
based upon the "actual" or "chance" frequency distribution resulting from a simple division into index-score
ranges on the basis of the response values assigned each
response (without any attempt being made to effect any
arbitrary "even" frequency distribution as was done with
the two-level "relative" index score).

Detailed explanations of each of the indices appear
on pages 23 through 36 of the coding outline, which
follow as pages 52 through 66 of this volume.

Several of the survey items in the questionnaire
which is reproduced as pages 29 through 48 of this
volume are phrased in the past tense, whereas in the
pre-election version of the questionnaire which was used
for the two groups of interviews conducted prior to the
1972 election they were phrased in the present tense.
These are questions 9 and 10 on page 11 and question 11
on page 12 of the questionnaire, which appear on pages
41 and 42 of this volume. The pre-election version of
each of these three questions is set out in its respective footnote.

The various survey items in the questionnaire (in the
form in which the questionnaire appears in this volume)
have been footnoted to indicate their respective sources.
The questionnaire in its original form (as used in the
survey) did not include either these footnotes or the
volume page numbers which have been assigned the pages
on which the questionnaire appears in this book.

West Georgia College

DIVISION OF THE UNIVERSITY SYSTEM OF GEORGIA

Carrollton, Georgia, 30117

Department of Political Science

Dear Student:

The following questionnaire, which you are being asked to answer, is being completed by a total of more than 10,000 college students currently enrolled in courses like yours at some fifty colleges and universities in eleven Southern states.

We think you will find the questions thought-provoking, interesting, and perhaps entertaining as well. Substantially all of the questions you are being asked are among the survey materials included in publications of the Survey Research Center of the Institute for Social Research at the University of Michigan. These survey items have been used at various times in a wide variety of surveys in this country.

You will note the appearance of numbers within some of the questions. Just disregard all numbers completely, since they are used only for convenience in tabulating your answers. Just check the space which corresponds with your answer to each question.

Please let us use this means to express our most sincere appreciation for your cooperation.

Very sincerely,

Dudley McClain
Assistant Professor of
Political Science

1. First, we would like some information relative to the political process.

   (a) Did you vote in the Presidential election in 1968?[1] (Check one.)

       (1) __ No   (2) __ Yes   (3) __ Too young

   (b) Are you presently registered to vote?[2]

       (1) __ No   (2) __ Yes

   (c) Have you ever been actively involved in any way in support of anyone's campaign for election to any public office?[3]

       (1) __ No   (2) __ Yes

   (d) Are you at present a member of any political party?[4]

       (1) __ No   (2) __ Yes

   (e) Generally speaking, which of the following would you say is the best way to describe your own identification with one of the political parties in this country at the present time? Do you consider yourself to be a/an:[5]

       (1) __ Strong Democrat
       (2) __ Not very strong Democrat
       (3) __ Independent, closer to the Dem. Party
       (4) __ Independent
       (5) __ Independent, closer to the Rep. Party
       (6) __ Not very strong Republican
       (7) __ Strong Republican
       (8) __ American Party
       (9) __ Other minor party (Please name:_____)

(f)   Suppose you had to classify yourself as either
      a conservative or a liberal, which would you
      say you are?[6]

      (1) __Conservative   (2) __ Liberal
      (3) __ Other (please specify): _____

2. Next, we would like you to look at the answer
    options beside the blank spaces for questions (a)
    through (e) below on this page and indicate your
    choices for each question by placing a check in the
    appropriate blank space for each question.

    (a)   First, please tell us how much you think you
          can trust the government in Washington to do
          what is right--just about always, most of the
          time, some of the time, or almost never?[7]

          (1)__almost never   (2)__some of the time
          (3)__most of the time (4)__just about always

    (b)   And how about your state government? How much
          do you think you can trust your state govern-
          ment to do what is right?[8]

          (1)__almost never   (2)__some of the time
          (3)__most of the time (4)__just about always

    (c)   How about your city government here? How much
          do you think you can trust your city government
          here to do what is right?[9]

          (1)__almost never   (2)__some of the time
          (3)__most of the time (4)__just about always

    (d)   Which of these officials would you say you
          could trust the most to do what is right--our
          president, your governor, or your mayor here?[10]

          (1)__president (2)__governor (3)__mayor

    (e)   And which of these officials would you say you
          could trust the least to do what is right--our
          president, your governor, or your mayor here?[11]

          (1)__president (2)__governor (3)__mayor

3. Now, we would like you to read (in the statements
    below) some of the different things that have been
    widely used in a large number of attitude and opin-
    ion surveys by others in this country and to tell us
    whether you agree or disagree with them. Just read
    each of the following statements one at a time, and
    check the answer that's closest to how you feel. By
    that we mean when you read each of these statements,
    just check the one of the four boxes that indicates
    whether you "agree a lot," "agree a little,"
    "disagree a little," or "disagree a lot."[12]

(NOTE: THE FOUR COLUMNS, OR "BOXES," WHICH APPEARED
TO THE RIGHT OF EACH STATEMENT ON THE QUESTIONNAIRE,
IN WHICH THE STUDENT WAS TO CHECK HIS ANSWER TO EACH,
HAVE BEEN DELETED IN THIS VOLUME TO SAVE SPACE.)

(a) I think of the government in Washington as the
     enemy rather than the friend of people like
     me.[13]

(b) I don't think public officials care much what
     people like me think.[14]

(c) Sometimes politics and government seem so com-
     plicated that a person like me can't understand
     what's going on.[15]

(d) Voting is the only way people like me can have
     any say about what the government does.[16]

(e) The way people vote is the main thing that
     decides how things are run in this country.[17]

(f) No one should ever be excused for breaking the
     law.[18]

(g) There are so many laws these days that it is
     asking too much to expect people to obey all
     of them.[19]

(h) It is better to obey a bad law and hope it will
     be changed than to disobey it.[20]

(i) We all suffer when people don't respect the
     law.[21]

(j) There are times when a person is justified in
     bending the law.[22]

(k) It's alright to disobey a law if it goes
     against your religion.[23]

(l) It is alright to break a law in an emergency
     like getting to the hospital in a hurry.[24]

(m) You cannot have justice unless people obey the
     law.[25]

(n) It's wrong to break a law, even though your
     conscience tells you the law is bad.[26]

(o) Most laws are for the good of the people.[27]

(p) If you start trying to change things very much,
     you usually make them worse.[28]

(q) If something grows up over a long time, there
     will always be much wisdom in it.[29]

(r) It's better to stick by what you have than to
     be trying new things you really don't know
     about.[30]

(s) We must respect the work of our forefathers and not think that we know better than they did.[31]

(t) A man really doesn't get to have much wisdom until he's well along in years.[32]

(u) These days a person doesn't really know who he can count on.[33]

(v) In spite of what some people say, the condition of the average man is getting worse, not better.[34]

(w) Sometimes I think people ought not to bring children into the world the way things look for the future.[35]

(x) Nowadays a person has to live pretty much for today and let tomorrow take care of itself.[36]

(y) There's not much use in people like me voting because all the candidates are usually against what I want.[37]

(z) The artist and the professor are probably more important than the businessman and the manufacturer.[38]

(aá) Human nature being what it is, there must always be war and conflict.[39]

(bb) What young people need most of all is strict discipline by their parents.[40]

(cc) Most people who don't get ahead just don't have enough will power.[41]

There are many groups and organizations in America that try to get the government or the American people to see things more their way. We would like to get your feelings toward some of these groups and organizations.

We have therefore included with this questionnaire this sheet of instructions on which is something called a "feeling thermometer." It is a device that has been used in a large number of surveys by others to measure peoples' feelings toward groups. NOW, CAREFULLY TEAR OUT THIS SHEET OF INSTRUCTIONS AND STUDY IT BEFORE GOING ON TO USE IT TO ANSWER QUESTIONS 4 AND 5 ON THE NEXT PAGE AND QUESTION 6 ON PAGE 7.

"FEELING THERMOMETER"[42]

(8) ___	100°	= Very warm or favorable feeling
(7) ___	85°	= Good, warm or favorable feeling
(6) ___	70°	= Fairly warm or favorable feeling
(5) ___	60°	= A bit more warm than cold
(9) ___	50°	= Don't know much about them
(4) ___	40°	= A bit more cold than warm
(3) ___	30°	= Fairly cold or unfavorable feeling
(2) ___	15°	= Quite cold or unfavorable feeling
(1) ___	0°	= Very cold or unfavorable feeling.

If you have a warm feeling toward a group, or feel favorably toward it, you would give it a score somewhere between 60° and 100° on this "thermometer," depending on how "warm" or "favorable" you feel toward the group.

On the other hand, if you don't feel very favorably toward some of these groups--that is, if there are some you don't care for too much or that you have a "cold" or "unfavorable" feeling toward--then you would place them somewhere between 0° and 40° on the "thermometer."

Now, we would like you to use the "feeling thermometer" to indicate your feelings, either "warm" or "cold," toward the groups and people listed on the next page. For each group, just write in the blank space the number of degrees that corresponds to your feelings about that particular group. If you just don't know or feel anything at all about the group or person, just check 50°.

4. Our first group is the American Legion. Where would
    you place them on the "feeling thermometer"? Just
    write in the blank space beside this group the num-
    ber of "degrees" that best indicates your feelings
    toward this group. Then repeat this procedure for
    all the other groups, writing in the blank beside
    each group the number of "degrees" that best indica-
    tes your feelings toward each separate group.[43]

    (a) _°American Legion   (k) _°John Birch Society
    (b) _°labor unions   (l) _°Women's liberation
    (c) _°Black Panthers   (m) _°government workers
    (d) _°college professors   (n) _°blue collar workers
    (e) _°National Guard   (o) _°policemen
    (f) _°Mexican-Americans   (p) _°Negroes
    (g) _°conservatives   (q) _°school teachers
    (h) _°Democrats   (r) _°Ku Klux Klan
    (i) _°Republicans   (s) _°whites
    (j) _°liberals   (t) _°the military

5. Next, still using the "feeling thermometer," please
    follow the same procedure and indicate your feelings
    toward each of the following people. Just write
    into the blank space beside each name the number of
    "degrees" that best describes how you feel about
    each person named.[44]

    (a) _°George Wallace   (m) _°Ronald Reagan
    (b) _°Edward Kennedy   (n) _°Lester Maddox
    (c) _°John Ashbrook   (o) _°George Meany
    (d) _°John Connolly   (p) _°Barry Goldwater
    (e) _°John Lindsay   (q) _°Henry Jackson
    (f) _°Angela Davis   (r) _°Hubert Humphrey
    (g) _°Spiro Agnew   (s) _°Eugene McCarthy
    (h) _°Wilbur Mills   (t) _°Vance Hartke
    (i) _°Richard Nixon   (u) _°Sam Yorty
    (j) _°Shirley Chisholm   (v) _°Paul McCloskey
    (k) _°George McGovern   (w) _°Terry Sanford
    (l) _°Edmund Muskie   (x) _°William F. Buckley

6. Now, we'd like for you to continue to use the
    "feeling thermometer" device and indicate your
    feelings about labor unions for certain groups.
    Just follow the same procedure you did for questions
    4 and 5 and write into the blank space beside each
    group the number of "degrees" that best describes
    how favorably or unfavorably you feel toward labor
    unions for each group listed.45

    (a) _°postal workers   (j) _°dock and warehouse
    (b) _°firemen   workers
    (c) _°phone co. workers   (k) _°government office
    (d) _°general laborers   workers
    (e) _°steel and aircraft   (l) _°policemen
        industry workers   (m) _°electric co. workers
    (f) _°military personnel   (n) _°farm laborers
    (g) _°school teachers   (o) _°truck drivers or
    (h) _°gas co. workers   teamsters
    (i) _°workers in the   (p) _°garbage workers
        building trades   (q) _°coal mine workers
                                (r) _°college professors

7. We would now like for you to go back to use of the
    four-column device, indicating, as you did before,
    whether you "agree" or "disagree" with a number of
    statements about yourself and your success in plan-
    ning ahead. Just check the block that corresponds
    to the answer that is closest to how you feel,
    indicating whether you "agree a lot," "agree a
    little," "disagree a little," or "disagree a lot"
    with each of these statements.

    (NOTE: THE FOUR COLUMNS, OR "BOXES," HAVE ALSO BEEN
    DELETED HERE TO FACILITATE SPACING IN THIS VOLUME.)

    (a) I would rather decide things when they come up
         than always try to plan ahead.46

    (b) I seem to be the kind of person that has more
         bad luck than good luck.47

    (c) There's not much use for me to plan ahead
         because there's usually something that makes
         me change my plans.48

    (d) I have often had the feeling that it's no use
         to try to get ahead in this life.49

8. Next, we'd like you to read some of the different
    things people have said about labor unions when
    they have been interviewed on other occasions. Just
    read each of the following statements one at a time
    and again <u>check</u> the block that corresponds to the
    answer that is <u>closest</u> to how <u>you</u> feel. Just check
    the <u>one</u> box for each statement that indicates
    whether you "<u>agree a lot</u>," "<u>agree a little</u>,"
    "<u>disagree a little</u>," or "<u>disagree a lot</u>" with each
    statement as you read it.

    (a) Steel workers, aircraft workers and others in
         industries like those should have the right to
         be in a labor union.[50]

    (b) Telephone, gas, and electric company employees
         should have the right to be in a labor union.[51]

    (c) The government ought to see to it that labor
         unions don't have much say about how the
         government is run.[52]

    (d) Government office workers should have the right
         to be in a labor union.[53]

    (e) Teachers should have the right to be in a
         labor union.[54]

    (f) Labor unions should become stronger and have
         more influence generally.[55]

    (g) Firemen and policemen should have the right to
         be in a labor union.[56]

    (h) General laborers should have the right to be in
         a labor union.[57]

    (i) Garbage workers should have the right to be in
         a labor union.[58]

(j)   Laws limiting the power of unions are just as necessary as laws designed to prevent abuses by big business.[59]

(k)   Post office workers should have the right to be in a labor union.[60]

(l)   Military personnel should have the right to be in a labor union.[61]

(m)   Labor unions are very necessary to protect the working man.[62]

(n)   Steel workers, aircraft workers and people like that should have the right to strike.[63]

(o)   Telephone, gas, and electric workers and people like that should have the right to strike.[64]

(p)   The government should do a lot more to regulate the activities of labor unions.[65]

(q)   Government office workers should have the right to strike.[66]

(r)   Teachers should have the right to strike.[67]

(s)   Workers should not have to join a union in order to hold a job.[68]

(t) Firemen and policemen should have the right to strike.[69]

(u) General laborers should have the right to strike.[70]

(v) If the majority of workers in a plant vote to have a union, the others should be required to join.[71]

(w) Military personnel should have the right to strike.[72]

(x) Post office workers should have the right to strike.[73]

(y) Trade unions do more harm than good to our industrial progress.[74]

(z) Most labor trouble is due to the work of radical agitators.[75]

(aa) Labor unions go too far when a boss can't fire his own workers.[76]

(bb) Garbage workers should have the right to strike.[77]

(cc) A general strike must be crushed at all costs.[78]

9. A large number of people at one time or another
    announced that they would seek the Democratic Party
    nomination for the Presidency in the 1972 election,
    or were considered prospects even though they may
    not have made any formal announcement that they were
    candidates for the nomination. The list included:
    (in alphabetical order) Shirley Chisholm, Vance
    Hartke, Hubert Humphrey, Henry Jackson, Edward
    Kennedy, John Lindsay, Eugene McCarthy, George
    McGovern, Lester Maddox, Wilbur Mills, Edmund
    Muskie, Terry Sanford, George Wallace and Sam
    Yorty. Of all of these who <u>were</u> in the running,
    which <u>one</u> would you have preferred to have seen get
    the Democratic Party nomination?[79]

    (1) ___Chisholm   (6) ___Lindsay   (11) ___Muskie
    (2) ___Hartke   (7) ___McCarthy   (12) ___Sanford
    (3) ___Humphrey   (8) ___McGovern   (13) ___Wallace
    (4) ___Jackson   (9) ___Maddox   (14) ___Yorty
    (5) ___Kennedy   (10) ___Mills

10. Below we have listed some of the possible Democratic
    Party nominees who <u>might</u> conceivably have run
    against the Republican Party nominee in 1972 in two-
    way races. For <u>each</u> <u>separate</u> <u>pairing</u> shown below,
    please check the name of the person you would have
    preferred to have seen elected President in 1972,
    <u>if</u> the race had been between those two individuals.[80]

    (1) ___Shirley Chisholm   OR   (2) ___Richard Nixon
    (1) ___Vance Hartke   OR   (2) ___Richard Nixon
    (1) ___Hubert Humphrey   OR   (2) ___Richard Nixon
    (1) ___Henry Jackson   OR   (2) ___Richard Nixon
    (1) ___Edward Kennedy   OR   (2) ___Richard Nixon
    (1) ___John Lindsay   OR   (2) ___Richard Nixon
    (1) ___Eugene McCarthy   OR   (2) ___Richard Nixon
    (1) ___George McGovern   OR   (2) ___Richard Nixon
    (1) ___Lester Maddox   OR   (2) ___Richard Nixon
    (1) ___Wilbur Mills   OR   (2) ___Richard Nixon
    (1) ___Edmund Muskie   OR   (2) ___Richard Nixon
    (1) ___Terry Sanford   OR   (2) ___Richard Nixon
    (1) ___George Wallace   OR   (2) ___Richard Nixon
    (1) ___Sam Yorty   OR   (2) ___Richard Nixon

11. Next, suppose the race for the Presidency had been
     a three-way race involving Richard Nixon as the
     Republican candidate, George Wallace as a third-
     party candidate, and the individual listed below
     in each instance as the Democratic candidate. For
     each of the following conceivable three-way races,
     check the one of the three candidates you would
     have preferred.[81]

     (1)__Chisholm   OR   (2)__Nixon   OR   (3)__Wallace
     (1)__Hartke   OR   (2)__Nixon   OR   (3)__Wallace
     (1)__Humphrey   OR   (2)__Nixon   OR   (3)__Wallace
     (1)__Jackson   OR   (2)__Nixon   OR   (3)__Wallace
     (1)__Kennedy   OR   (2)__Nixon   OR   (3)__Wallace
     (1)__Lindsay   OR   (2)__Nixon   OR   (3)__Wallace
     (1)__McCarthy   OR   (2)__Nixon   OR   (3)__Wallace
     (1)__McGovern   OR   (2)__Nixon   OR   (3)__Wallace
     (1)__Maddox   OR   (2)__Nixon   OR   (3)__Wallace
     (1)__Mills   OR   (2)__Nixon   OR   (3)__Wallace
     (1)__Muskie   OR   (2)__Nixon   OR   (3)__Wallace
     (1)__Sanford   OR   (2)__Nixon   OR   (3)__Wallace
     (1)__Yorty   OR   (2)__Nixon   OR   (3)__Wallace

Last, we would like some background information on you
and your family. Then you will have completed the
interview.

12. First, please check the space beside the range of
     years that includes your age. Just check the
     category below which includes your age at present.[82]

     (1)____18-25   (6)____45-49
     (2)____26-29   (7)____50-59
     (3)____30-34   (8)____60-64
     (4)____35-39   (9)____65 and over
     (5)____40-44

13. Are you married now and living with your husband
    or wife--or are you single, divorced, separated,
    or what?[83]

    (1) ___married   (4) ___widowed
    (2) ___divorced   (5) ___separated
    (3) ___single   (6) ___common-law

14. In what state is your "home town" or your place
    of "permanent" residence located?[84]

(41) ___ Ala.	(45) ___ La.	(24) ___ Ohio
(81) ___ Alaska	(02) ___ Maine	(53) ___ Okla.
(61) ___ Ariz.	(52) ___ Md.	(72) ___ Ore.
(42) ___ Ark.	(03) ___ Mass.	(14) ___ Pa.
(71) ___ Calif.	(23) ___ Mich.	(05) ___ R. I.
(62) ___ Colo.	(33) ___ Minn.	(48) ___ S. C.
(01) ___ Conn.	(46) ___ Miss.	(37) ___ S. D.
(11) ___ Del.	(34) ___ Mo.	(54) ___ Tenn.
(55) ___ D. C.	(64) ___ Mont.	(49) ___ Tex.
(43) ___ Fla.	(35) ___ Nebr.	(67) ___ Utah
(44) ___ Ga.	(65) ___ Nev.	(06) ___ Vt.
(82) ___ Hawaii	(04) ___ N. H.	(40) ___ Va.
(63) ___ Idaho	(12) ___ N. J.	(73) ___ Wash.
(21) ___ Ill.	(66) ___ N. M.	(56) ___ W. Va.
(22) ___ Ind.	(13) ___ N. Y.	(25) ___ Wisc.
(31) ___ Iowa	(47) ___ N. C.	(68) ___ Wyo.
(32) ___ Kan.	(36) ___ N. D.	(99) ___ Foreign
(51) ___ Ky.		

15. Next, would you please tell us the size of the population of the community you consider to be your "home town" or "permanent" residence. By that we mean the overall size of the locality, and not necessarily the population within the city limits. In a metropolitan area such as Atlanta, Georgia, for example, if you lived in the suburb of Sandy Springs or Forest Park, neither of which might have as much as 100,000 population, you should still indicate the size of the larger metropolitan area within which you live, which would be "greater than 1 million."[85]

(1) ___   1- 2,499   (5) ___ 100,000-249,999
(2) ___   2,500- 9,999   (6) ___ 250,000-449,999
(3) ___ 10,000-24,999   (7) ___ 500,000- 1 million
(4) ___ 25,000-99,999   (8) ___ more than 1 million

16. As things now stand, how many years of formal or "higher" education do you think you will want to complete? By that we mean what is the highest degree you think you want to earn?[86]

(1) ___ no degree   (4) ___ Ph.D.
(2) ___ bachelors   (5) ___ professional
(3) ___ masters   (6) ___ other: (_____)

17. How many years of college education have you completed so far. By that we mean, in which year of college work are you now?[87]

(1) ___ freshman   (4) ___ senior
(2) ___ sophomore   (5) ___ masters (specify
(3) ___ junior   field): _____

18. How many years of education did your father complete?[88]

(1) ___ none
(2) ___ grade school only
(3) ___ some high school
(4) ___ completed high school
(5) ___ completed high school, + non-college study
(6) ___ some college, but no degree
(7) ___ college bachelors (4 years) degree
(8) ___ college bachelors degree, + masters degree
(9) ___ college bachelors degree, + Ph.D. or
        professional degree

19. How many years of education did your mother complete?[89]

    (1) ___ none
    (2) ___ grade school only
    (3) ___ some high school
    (4) ___ completed high school
    (5) ___ completed high school, + non-college study
    (6) ___ some college, but no degree
    (7) ___ college bachelors (4 year) degree
    (8) ___ college bachelors + masters degree
    (9) ___ college bachelors degree, + Ph. D or
            professional degree

20. Please check the category below that best indicates the school or area of study in which you are presently enrolled in college. By that is meant the school or area on the list below that is closest to the classification of the school or area in which you are now enrolled.[90]

    (1) ___Agriculture   (6) ___Graduate School
    (2) ___Arts and Sciences (7) ___Home Economics
    (3) ___Business Admin. (8) ___Nursing
    (4) ___Education   (9) ___Other (Please
    (5) ___Engineering   specify) _____

21. As things now stand, in which of the following occupational areas do you think you will work after you complete your schooling?[91]

    (1) _Profession, Technical, or the like.
    (2) _Mgr., Official, Proprietor (not Farm), Retail.
    (3) _Clerical, Secretarial, Salesman.
    (4) _Craftsman, Foreman, Mechanic, or the like.
    (5) _Machinery Operator, Driver, and the like.
    (6) _Household or Service Worker, Military, Police.
    (7) _Laborer (not Farm or Mine), Teamster,
        Warehouseman.
    (8) _Farmer, Farm Manager, Farm Foreman or Worker.
    (9) _Not expect to be in labor force at all.

22. In which of the following occupational areas is the person who is head of your household employed? By "head of your household" is meant the one of your parents who is the principal "breadwinner" for your family, unless you are yourself your primary means of support, your own "breadwinner," and not supported by either or both of your parents.[92]

   (1) _Profession, Technical, or the like.
   (2) _Mgr., Official, Proprietor (not Farm), Retail.
   (3) _Clerical, Secretarial, Salesman.
   (4) _Craftsman, Foreman, Mechanic, or the like.
   (5) _Machinery Operator, Driver, and the like.
   (6) _Household or Service Worker, Military, Police.
   (7) _Laborer (not Farm or Mine), Teamster, Warehouseman.
   (8) _Farmer, Farm Manager, Farm Foreman or Worker.
   (9) _Not expect to be in labor force at all.

23. Is the head of your household self-employed?[93]

   (1) ___ Yes   (2) ___ No

24. Which of the following best describes the primary employment status of the head of your household?[94]

   (1) ___ Employed
   (2) ___ Unemployed, laid off, or sick
   (3) ___ Retired
   (4) ___ Permanently disabled (under 65)
   (5) ___ Housewife
   (6) ___ Student
   (7) ___ Other (specify): _____

25. IF YOU ARE A MALE: Are you a veteran?[95]

   (1) ___ Yes   (2) ___ No

   IF YOU ARE A MARRIED FEMALE: Is your husband a veteran?

   (3) ___ Yes   (4) ___ No

   IF YOU ARE A SINGLE FEMALE: Simply check this space: (5) _____

26. Does anyone in your immediate family belong to a labor union?[96]

   ___Yes   (1)___No

   IF YOUR ANSWER TO QUESTION 26, ABOVE, IS "YES,"
   PLEASE INDICATE THEIR RELATIONSHIP TO YOU.
   (2)___myself   (5)___my brother/sister
   (3)___my husband/wife   (6)___parent
   (4)___my child   (7)___other (specify)____

27. Please indicate below the answer that most closely reflects your church attendance, or your position with respect to religion.[97]

   (1)___Protestant   (5)___No organized church
   (2)___Catholic   (6)___Agnostic
   (3)___Jewish   (7)___Atheist
   (4)___Other:_____

28. Would you say you go to church regularly, often, seldom, or never?[98]

   (1)_regularly (2)_often (3)_seldom (4)_never

29. American social scientists have made studies which indicate that there are several major social classes in our society. In which of the following social classes would you say your family belongs?[99] (Just check one)

   (1)___lower   (4)___middle-middle
   (2)___working   (5)___upper-middle
   (3)___lower-middle   (6)___upper

30. Please indicate below your sex:

   (1)___female   (2)___male

31. Please indicate below the racial or ethnic group of which you are a member.[100]

   (1)_American Indian   (4)_Oriental-American
   (2)_Anglo-American   (5)_Spanish-surnamed
   (3)_Black-American   American
                                (6)_"Foreign" student

32. Do your parents (or you and your husband or wife, <u>if</u> you are married and living separately from your parents' household <u>and</u> <u>if</u> you and your husband or wife are completely self-supporting) own their (or your) own home, or rent, or what?[101]

    (1) _own it   (2) _rent   (3)_other:_____

33. About what do you think your total family income (before taxes) was for yourself and your immediate family for last year? By that we mean your parents' total income if they are the primary "breadwinners" on whom you depend for your livelihood, or yourself, or yourself and your spouse if you are completely self-supported and are not dependent upon your parents for any of your support. Just check the blank space that corresponds to the correct income category.[102]

(01) ___ under $1,000		(09) ___ $ 8,000-$ 8,999	
(02) ___ $1,000-$1,999		(10) ___ $ 9,000-$ 9,999	
(03) ___ $2,000-$2,999		(11) ___ $10,000-$11,999	
(04) ___ $3,000-$3,999		(12) ___ $12,000-$14,999	
(05) ___ $4,000-$4,999		(13) ___ $15,000-$19,999	
(06) ___ $5,000-$5,999		(14) ___ $20,000-$24,999	
(07) ___ $6,000-$6,999		(15) ___ $25,000-$49,999	
(08) ___ $7,000-$7,999		(16) ___ $50,000 and over	

The last thing we would like to ask you is your impression of our last two Presidents.

34. Some people say President Nixon is not a real Republican. Is he the kind of man <u>you</u> think of as being a real Republican?[103]

    (1) ___ Yes   (2) ___ No

35. Some people also say that while he was in office President Lyndon Johnson was not a real Democrat. As President, was he the kind of man <u>you</u> think of as being a real Democrat?[104]

    (1) ___ Yes   (2) ___ No

That completes the interview. Thank you very much for your cooperation. We appreciate it very much.

NOTE: THE DATA WHICH ARE DESCRIBED ON THE REMAINING
PAGES OF THIS CODING OUTLINE WERE DERIVED THROUGH RE-
CODING OF DATA FROM OTHER DATA LOCATIONS, THROUGH A
LISTING BY STATE OF THE SCHOOLS WHICH WERE INVOLVED
IN THE STUDY, AND FROM TOTALING AND AVERAGING AND
COMPUTING INDEX SCORES FOR THE RESPONSES TO THE SEVERAL
SERIES OF ATTITUDINAL MEASURES. WHERE THESE ADDITIONAL
DATA ARE DIRECTLY RELATED TO SOME QUESTION WHICH CAN
BE IDENTIFIED BY QUESTION NUMBER, THIS HAS BEEN DONE
BY REPEATING THE QUESTION NUMBER. WHERE THESE DATA
CANNOT BE DIRECTLY RELATED TO ONE OF THE QUESTIONS ON
THE SURVEY INSTRUMENT, THE DESCRIPTION OF THE ADDITIONAL
VARIABLE SO CREATED HAS NOT BEEN PRECEDED BY ANY NUMBER.

1(e). Pro-Democratic Party Identification.
  (1) Strong Republican
  (2) Not very strong Republican
  (3) Independent, closer to the Republican Party
  (4) Independent
  (5) Independent, closer to the Democratic Party
  (6) Not very strong Democrat
  (7) Strong Democrat
  (8) American Party
  (9) Other minority party

Institutions at which enrolled, by state: Alabama.
  (1) Alabama A. & M. Univ., Normal, Ala.
  (2) Auburn Univ., Auburn, Ala.
  (3) Jacksonville State Univ., Jacksonville, Ala.
  (4) Univ. of Montevallo, Montevallo, Ala.

Institutions at which enrolled, by state: Arkansas.
  (1) Arkansas Polytechnic College, Russellville, Ark.
  (2) State College of Arkansas, Conway, Ark.
  (3) Univ. of Arkansas, Fayetteville, Ark.
  (4) Univ. of Arkansas at Pine Bluff, Pine Bluff, Ark.

Institutions at which enrolled, by state: Florida.
  (1) Florida A. & M Univ., Tallahassee, Fla.
  (2) Florida State Univ., Tallahassee, Fla.
  (3) Univ. of South Florida, Tampa, Fla.

Institutions at which enrolled, by state: Georgia.
(1) Albany State College, Albany, Ga.
(2) Columbus College, Columbus, Ga.
(3) DeKalb Community College, Clarkston, Ga.
(4) Georgia Institute of Technology, Atlanta, Ga.
(5) Georgia State Univ., Atlanta, Ga.
(6) North Georgia College, Dahlonega, Ga.
(7) Valdosta State College, Valdosta, Ga.
(8) West Georgia College, Carrollton, Ga.

Institutions at which enrolled, by state: Louisiana.
(1) Grambling College, Grambling, La.
(2) Louisiana State Univ., Baton Rouge, La.
(3) Louisiana Tech Univ., Ruston, La.
(4) Northeast Louisiana Univ., Monroe, La.

Institutions at which enrolled, by state: Mississippi.
(1) Jackson State College, Jackson, Miss.
(2) Mississippi State Univ., State College, Miss.
(3) Univ. of Mississippi, University, Miss.
(4) Univ. of Southern Mississippi, Hattiesburg, Miss.

Institutions at which enrolled by state: North Carolina.
(1) East Carolina Univ., Greenville, N. C.
(2) North Carolina A. & T. Univ., Greensboro, N. C.
(3) North Carolina Central Univ., Durham, N. C.
(4) Univ. of North Carolina, Chapel Hill, N. C.
(5) Western Carolina Univ., Cullowhee, N. C.

Institutions at which enrolled by state: South Carolina.
(1) Clemson Univ., Clemson, S. C.
(2) College of Charleston, Charleston, S. C.
(3) South Carolina State College, Orangeburg, S. C.
(4) Univ. of South Carolina, Columbia, S. C.

Institutions at which enrolled, by state: Tennessee.
(1) Memphis State Univ., Memphis, Tenn.
(2) Middle Tennessee State Univ., Murphreesboro, Tenn.
(3) Tennessee State Univ., Nashville, Tenn.
(4) Tennessee Technological Univ., Cookeville, Tenn.
(5) Univ. of Tennessee, Knoxville, Tenn.

Institutions at which enrolled, by state: Texas.
   (1) Sam Houston State Univ., Huntsville, Tex.
   (2) Texas Southern Univ., Houston, Tex.
   (3) Texas Tech Univ., Lubbock, Tex.
   (4) Univ. of Texas at Arlington, Arlington, Tex.
   (5) West Texas State Univ., Canyon, Tex.

Institutions at which enrolled, by state: Virginia:
   (1) Norfolk State Univ., Norfolk, Va.
   (2) Univ. of Virginia, Charlottesville, Va.
   (3) Virginia Commonwealth Univ., Richmond, Va.
   (4) Virginia Polytechnic Univ., Blacksburg, Va.

33. Perception of family income level (recoded from Q. 33,
    page 18.)
   (1) $ 0-$ 2,999.   (5) $15,000-$24,999.
   (2) $ 3,000-$ 6,999.   (6) $25,000-$49,999.
   (3) $ 7,000-$ 9,999.   (7) $50,000 and over.
   (4) $10,000-$14,999.

Interview Group (which of four times R was interviewed):
   (1) Group   I: Spring, 1972, prior to 1972 election.
   (2) Group   II: Fall, 1972, prior to 1972 election.
   (3) Group III: Spring, 1973, after 1972 election.
   (4) Group   IV: Fall, 1973, after 1972 election.

Classification of institutions as either "minority" or
"non-minority":
   (1) Minority school (predominantly black student body)
   (2) Non-minority school (predominantly white student
      body)

Whether interview before or after 1972 election and
discovery of Watergate:
   (1) In Group I or II and interviewed before election,
      Watergate.
   (2) In Group III or IV and interviewed after election,
      Watergate.

PARTICIPATION INDEX SCORE (Questions 1b-1d):

   Index score based upon summation of respondent's
scores on the three participation items. Items summed,
and index score determined for each respondent, only if
all three items were answered. Zero value punched if
fewer than all three items were answered. Index score
determined on basis of summation of the respondent's
answers to the three participation items, with the
index score assigned being dependent upon where that
total score fell within specified ranges of scores on
the three items, as follows:

(0) - None answered or some, but not all, answered.
(1) - Score between 3 and 3 = NO participation.
(2) - Score between 4 and 4 = SLIGHT participation.
(3) - Score between 5 and 5 = MODERATE participation.
(4) - Score between 6 and 6 = HIGH participation.

   NOTE: Question item 1(a) was not included with other
three participation items in this computation, since
item 1(a) had a third answer option and would not,
therefore, be appropriate for inclusion in a "four-level"
participation index score.

TRUST INDEX SCORE (RELATIVE), 4 LEVELS (Q. 2a, 2b, 3a):

Index score based upon summation of respondent's
scores on the three trust items noted. Items summed,
and index score determined for each respondent, only
if all three items were answered. Zero value punched
if fewer than all three items were answered. Index
scores determined on basis of summation of the respondent's answers to the three trust items, with the index
score assigned being dependent upon where that total
score fell within specified ranges of scores on the
three items, as follows:

(0) – None answered or some, but not all, answered.
(1) – Score between 3 and 6 = LOW trust.
(2) – Score between 7 and 8 = SLIGHT trust.
(3) – Score between 9 and 9 = MODERATE trust.
(4) – Score between 10 and 12 = HIGH trust.

NOTE: Question 2c was not included because it did
not correlate positively with the other three items
which were included; items 2d and 2e were not included
because they did not measure degrees of trust.

TRUST INDEX SCORE (RELATIVE), 2 LEVELS (Q. 2a, 2b, 3a):

Index score based upon summation of respondent's
score on three trust items and computed in manner described for computation of four-level trust index score
above, except that only two levels of trust are defined
in this trust index score.

(0) – None answered or some, but not all, answered.
(1) – Score between 3 and 8 = Not trusting.
(2) – Score between 9 and 12 = Trusting.

NOTE: Question items 2c, 2d and 2e were not included
in determination of two-level trust index score. Item
2d was not included because it did not correlate
positively with the other three items which were included; items 2d and 2e were not included because they did
not measure degrees of trust.

EFFICACY INDEX SCORE (RELATIVE), 4 Levels (Q. 3b-3d):

   Index score based upon summation of respondent's
scores on the three efficacy items noted. Items summed,
and index score determined for each respondent, only
if all three items were answered. Zero value punched
if fewer than all three items were answered. Index
scores determined on basis of summation of the respondent's answers to the three efficacy items, with the
index score assigned being dependent upon where that
total score fell within specified ranges of scores on
the three items, as follows:

(0) - None answered or some, but not all, answered.
(1) - Score between 4 and 8 = LOW efficacy.
(2) - Score between 9 and 10 = SLIGHT efficacy.
(3) - Score between 11 and 12 = MODERATE efficacy.
(4) - Score between 13 and 16 = HIGH efficacy.

   NOTE: Question 3(e) was not included with the other
three efficacy items in this computation, since it did
not correlate positively with them.

EFFICACY INDEX SCORE (RELATIVE), 2 LEVELS (Q. 3b-3d):

   Index score based upon summation of respondent's
scores on the three efficacy items and computed in
manner described for computation of four-level efficacy
index score above, except that only two levels of
efficacy are defined in this efficacy index score.

(0) - None answered or some, but not all, answered.
(1) - Score between 3 and 10 = Not efficacious.
(2) - Score between 11 and 16 = Efficacious.

   NOTE: Question 3(e) was not included with the other
three efficacy items in this computation, since it did
not correlate positively with them.

OBLIGATION INDEX SCORE (RELATIVE, 4 LEVELS (Q. 3f-3o):

   Index score based upon summation of respondent's
scores on the nine obligation items noted.   Items summed,
and index score determined for each respondent, only if
all nine items were answered.   Zero value punched if
fewer than all nine items were answered.   Index scores
determined on basis of summation of the respondent's
answers to the nine obligation items, with the index
score assigned being dependent upon where that total
score fell within specified ranges of scores on the
nine items, as follows:

(0) - None answered or some, but not all, answered.
(1) - Score between 9 and 21 = LOW obligation.
(2) - Score between 22 and 24 = SLIGHT obligation.
(3) - Score between 25 and 28 = MODERATE obligation.
(4) - Score between 29 and 36 = HIGH obligation.

   NOTE: Question 3(1) was not included with the other
nine obligation items in this computation, since it
did not correlate positively with them.

OBLIGATION INDEX SCORE (RELATIVE), 2 LEVELS (Q. 3f-3o):

   Index score based upon summation of respondent's
scores on the nine included obligation items and computed
in the manner described for computation of four-level
obligation index score above, except that only two levels
of obligation, or law-abidingness, are defined in this
obligation index score.

(0) - None answered or some, but not all, answered.
(1) - Score between 9 and 24 = Not obligated.
(2) - Score between 25 and 36 = Obligated.

   NOTE: Question 3(1) was not included with the other
nine obligation items in this computation, since it did
not correlate positively with them.

PERSONAL CONSERVATISM INDEX SCORE (RELATIVE), 4 LEVELS
    (Q. 3p-3t):

Index score based upon summation of respondent's
scores on the five personal conservatism items noted.
Items summed, and index score determined for each
respondent, only if all five items were answered.   Zero
value punched if fewer than all five were answered.
Index scores determined on basis of summation of the
respondent's answers to the five personal conservatism
items, with the index score assigned being dependent
upon where that total score fell within specified
ranges of scores on the five items, as follows:

(0) - None answered or some, but not all, answered.
(1) - Score between 5 and 7 = LOW conservatism.
(2) - Score between 8 and 9 = SLIGHT conservatism.
(3) - Score between 10 and 11 = MODERATE conservatism.
(4) - Score between 12 and 20 = HIGH conservatism.

NOTE: All five items in the personal conservatism
series were included in this computation, since all five
correlated positively.

PERSONAL CONSERVATISM INDEX SCORE (RELATIVE), 2 LEVELS
    (Q. 3p-3t):

Index score based upon summation of respondent's
scores on the five personal conservatism items and
computed in the manner described for computation of
the four-level personal conservatism index scores above,
except that only two levels of personal conservatism are
defined in this personal conservatism index score.

(0) - None answered or some, but not all, answered.
(1) - Score between 5 and 9 = Not conservative.
(2) - Score between 10 and 20 = Conservative.

NOTE: All five items in the personal conservatism
series were included in this computation, since all five
correlated positively.

ALIENATION INDEX SCORE (RELATIVE), 4 LEVELS (Q. 3u-3y):

Index score based upon summation of respondent's scores on the five alienation items noted. Items summed, and index score determined for each respondent, only if all five items were answered. Zero value punched if fewer than all five were answered. Index scores determined on basis of summation of the respondent's answers to the five personal alienation items, with the index score assigned being dependent upon where that total score fell within specified ranges of scores on the five items, as follows:

(0) — None answered or some, but not all, answered.
(1) — Score between 5 and 9 = LOW alienation.
(2) — Score between 10 and 11 = SLIGHT alienation.
(3) — Score between 12 and 13 = MODERATE alienation.
(4) — Score between 14 and 20 = HIGH alienation.

NOTE: All five items in the alienation series were included in this computation, since all five correlated positively.

ALIENATION INDEX SCORE (RELATIVE), 2 LEVELS (Q. 3u-3y):

Index score based upon summation of respondent's scores on the five alientation items and computed in the manner described for computation of the four-level alienation index score above, except that only two levels of alienation are defined in this two-level alienation index score.

(0) — None answered or some, but not all, answered.
(1) — Score between 5 and 11 = Not alienated.
(2) — Score between 12 and 20 = Alienated.

NOTE: All five items in the alienation series were included in this computation, since all five correlated positively.

AUTHORITARIANISM INDEX SCORE (RELATIVE), 4 LEVELS
(Q. 3aa-3cc):

Index score based upon summation of respondent's
scores on the three authoritarianism items which were
included in the series for the purpose of this computation. Items summed, and index score determined for
each respondent, only if all three items were answered.
Zero value punched if fewer than all three items were
answered. Index scores determined on basis of summation
of the respondent's answers to the three authoritarianism items, with the index score assigned being dependent upon where that total score fell within specified
ranges of scores on the three items, as follows:

(0) - None answered or some, but not all, answered.
(1) - Score between 3 and 5 = LOW authoritarianism.
(2) - Score between 6 and 7 = SLIGHT authoritarianism.
(3) - Score between 8 and 9 = MODERATE authoritarianism.
(4) - Score between 10 and 12 = HIGH authoritarianism.

NOTE: Question 3z was not included with the other
three authoritarianism items in this computation, since
it did not correlate positively with them.

AUTHORITARIANISM INDEX SCORE (RELATIVE), 2 LEVELS
(Q. 3aa-3cc):

Index score based upon summation of respondent's
scores on the three included authoritarianism items and
computed in the manner described for computation of
four-level authoritarianism index score above, except
that only two levels of authoritarianism are defined in
this authoritarianism index score.

(0) - None answered or some, but not all, answered.
(1) - Score between 3 and 7 = Not authoritarian.
(2) - Score between 8 and 12 = Authoritarian.

NOTE: Question 3z was not included with the other
three authoritarianism items in this computation, since
it did not correlate positively with them.

PERSONAL CYNICISM INDEX SCORE (RELATIVE), 4 LEVELS
   (Q. 7a-7d):

   Index score based upon summation of respondent's
scores on the four personal cynicism items.   Items
summed, and index score determined for each respondent,
only if all four items were answered.   Zero value punched if fewer than all four were answered.   Index scores
determined on basis of summation of the respondent's
answers to the four personal cynicism items, with the
index score assigned being dependent upon where that
total score fell within specified ranges of scores on
the four items, as follows:

(0) - None answered or some, but not all, answered.
(1) - Score between 4 and 6 = LOW personal cynicism.
(2) - Score between 7 and 8 = SLIGHT personal cynicism.
(3) - Score between 9 and 10 = MODERATE personal
                                cynicism.
(4) - Score between 11 and 16 = HIGH personal cynicism.

   NOTE: All four items in the personal cynicism series
were included in this computation, since all correlated
positively.

PERSONAL CYNICISM INDEX SCORE (RELATIVE), 2 LEVELS
   (Q. 7a-7d):

   Index score based upon summation of respondent's
scores on the four personal cynicism items and computed
in the manner described for computation of the four-level
personal cynicism index score above, except that only two
levels of personal cynicism are defined in this personal
cynicism index score.

(0) - None answered or some, but not all, answered.
(1) - Score between 4 and 8 = Not cynical.
(2) - Score between 9 and 16 = Cynical.

   NOTE: All four items in the personal cynicism series
were included in this computation, since all four
correlated positively.

TRUST INDEX SCORE .(ABSOLUTE), 4 LEVELS (Q. 2a, 2b, 3a):

Index score based upon summation of respondent's scores on the three trust items noted. Items summed, and index score determined for each respondent, only if all three items were answered. Zero value punched if fewer than all three items were answered. Index scores determined on basis of summation of the respondent's answers to the three trust items, with the index score assigned being dependent upon where that total score fell within specified ranges of scores on the three items, as follows:

(0) - None answered or some, but not all, answered.
(1) - Score between 3 and 4 = LOW trust.
(2) - Score between 5 and 7 = SLIGHT trust.
(3) - Score between 8 and 10 = MODERATE trust.
(4) - Score between 11 and 12 = HIGH trust.

NOTE: Question items 2c, 2d and 2e were not included in the determination of the four-level index score. Item 2c was not included because it did not correlate positively with the other three items which were included; items 2d and 2e were not included because they did not measure degrees of trust.

TRUST INDEX SCORE (ABSOLUTE), 2 LEVELS (Q. 2a, 2b, 3a):

Index score based upon summation of respondent's scores on the three trust items and computed in manner described for computation of four-level trust index score above, except that only two levels of trust are defined in this trust index score.

(0) - None answered or some, but not all, answered.
(1) - Score between 3 and 7 = Not trusting.
(2) - Score between 8 and 12 = Trusting.

NOTE: Question items 2c, 2d and 2e were not included in determination of two-level trust index score. Item 2c was not included because it did not correlate positively with the other three items which were included; items 2d and 2e were not included because they did not measure degrees of trust.

EFFICACY INDEX SCORE (ABSOLUTE), 4 LEVELS (Q. 3b-3d):

   Index score based upon summation of respondent's
scores on three of the efficacy items noted. Items
summed, and index score determined for each respondent,
only if all three items were answered. Zero value
punched if fewer than all three items were answered.
Index scores determined on basis of summation of the
respondent's answers to the three efficacy items, with
the index score assigned being dependent upon where that
total score fell within specified ranges of scores on
the three items, as follows:

(0) - None answered or some, but not all, answered.
(1) - Score between 3 and 4 = LOW efficacy.
(2) - Score between 5 and 7 = SLIGHT efficacy.
(3) - Score between 8 and 10 = MODERATE efficacy.
(4) - Score between 11 and 12 = HIGH efficacy.

   NOTE: Question item 3d was not included with the
other three efficacy items in this computation, since
item 3d did not correlate positively with them.

EFFICACY INDEX SCORE (ABSOLUTE), 2 LEVELS (Q. 3b-3d):

   Index score based upon summation of respondent's
scores on three of the efficacy items and computed in
manner described for computation of four-level efficacy
index score above, except that only two levels of
efficacy are defined in this efficacy index score.

(0) - None answered or some, but not all, answered.
(1) - Score between 3 and 7 = Not efficacious.
(2) - Score between 8 and 12 = Efficacious.

   NOTE: Question item 3d was not included with the
other three efficacy items in this computation, since
item 3d did not correlate positively with them.

OBLIGATION INDEX SCORE (ABSOLUTE), 4 LEVELS (Q. 3f-3o):

Index score based upon summation of respondent's scores on the nine obligation items noted. Items summed, and index score determined for each respondent, only if all nine items were answered. Zero value punched if fewer than all nine items were answered. Index scores determined on basis of summation of the respondent's answers to the nine obligation items, with the index score assigned being dependent upon where that total score fell within specified ranges of scores on the nine items, as follows:

(0) - None answered or some, but not all, answered.
(1) - Score between 9 and 13 = LOW obligation.
(2) - Score between 14 and 22 = SLIGHT obligation.
(3) - Score between 23 and 31 = MODERATE obligation.
(4) - Score between 32 and 36 = HIGH obligation.

NOTE: Question 3(1) was not included with the other nine obligation items in this computation, since it did not correlate positively with them.

OBLIGATION INDEX SCORE (ABSOLUTE), 2 LEVELS (Q. 3f-3o):

Index score based upon summation of respondent's scores on the nine included obligation items and computed in the manner described for computation of four-level obligation index score above, except that only two levels of obligation, or law-abidingness, are defined in this obligation index score.

(0) - None answered or some, but not all, answered.
(1) - Score between 9 and 22 = Not obligated.
(2) - Score between 23 and 36 = Obligated.

NOTE: Question 3(1) was not included with the other nine obligation items in this computation, since it did not correlate positively with them.

PERSONAL CONSERVATISM INDEX SCORE (ABSOLUTE), 4 LEVELS
    (Q. 3p-3t):

   Index score based upon summation of respondent's
scores on the five personal conservatism items noted.
Items summed, and index score determined for each
respondent, only if all five items were answered. Zero
value punched if fewer than all five were answered.
Index scores determined on basis of summation of the
respondent's answers to the five personal conservatism
items, with the index score assigned being dependent
upon where that total score fell within specified ranges
of scores on the five items, as follows:

(0) - None answered or some, but not all, answered.
(1) - Score between 5 and 7 = LOW conservatism.
(2) - Score between 8 and 12 = SLIGHT conservatism.
(3) - Score between 13 and 17 = MODERATE conservatism.
(4) - Score between 18 and 20 = HIGH conservatism.

   NOTE: All five items in the personal conservatism
series were included in this computation, since all
five correlated positively.

PERSONAL CONSERVATISM INDEX SCORE (ABSOLUTE), 2 LEVELS
    (Q. 3p-3t):

   Index score based upon summation of respondent's
scores on the five personal conservatism items and
computed in the manner described for computation of the
four-level personal conservatism index score above,
except that only two levels of personal conservatism are
defined in this personal conservatism index score.

(0) - None answered or some, but not all, answered.
(1) - Score between 5 and 12 = Not conservative.
(2) - Score between 13 and 20 = Conservative.

   NOTE: All five items in the personal conservatism
series were included in this computation, since all five
correlated positively.

ALIENATION INDEX SCORE (ABSOLUTE), 4 LEVELS (Q. 3u-3y):

Index score based upon summation of respondent's scores on the five alienation items noted. Items summed, and index score determined for each respondent, only if all five items were answered. Zero value punched if fewer than all five were answered. Index scores determined on basis of summation of the respondent's answers to the five personal alienation items, with the index score assigned being dependent upon where that total score fell within specified ranges of scores on the five items, as follows:

(0) - None answered or some, but not all, answered.
(1) - Score between 5 and 7 = LOW alienation.
(2) - Score between 8 and 12 = SLIGHT alienation.
(3) - Score between 13 and 17 = MODERATE alienation.
(4) - Score between 18 and 20 = HIGH alienation.

NOTE: All five items in the alienation series were included in this computation, since all five correlated positively.

ALIENATION INDEX SCORE (ABSOLUTE), 2 LEVELS (Q. 3u-3y):

Index score based upon summation of respondent's scores on the five alienation items and computed in the manner described for computation of the four-level alienation index score above, except that only two levels of alienation are defined in this two-level alienation index score.

(0) - None answered or some, but not all, answered.
(1) - Score between 5 and 12 = Not alientated.
(2) - Score between 13 and 20 = Alienated.

NOTE: All five items in the alienation series were included in this computation, since all five correlated positively.

AUTHORITARIANISM INDEX SCORE (ABSOLUTE), 4 LEVELS
(3aa-3cc):

Index score based upon summation of respondent's
scores on the three authoritarianism items which were
included in the series for the purpose of this computation. Items summed, and index score determined for
each respondent, only if all three items were answered.
Zero value punched if fewer than all three items were
answered. Index scores determined on basis of summation
of the respondent's answers to the three authoritarianism items, with the index score assigned being dependent
upon where that total score fell within specified ranges
of scores on the three items, as follows:

(0) - None answered or some, but not all, answered.
(1) - Score between 3 and 4 = LOW authoritarianism.
(2) - Score between 5 and 7 = SLIGHT authoritarianism.
(3) - Score between 8 and 10 = MODERATE authoritarian-
                                ism.
(4) - Score between 11 and 12 = HIGH authoritarianism.

NOTE: Question 3z was not included with the other
three authoritarianism items in this computation, since
it did not correlate positively with them.

AUTHORITARIANISM INDEX SCORE (ABSOLUTE), 2 LEVELS
(Q. 3aa-3cc):

Index score based upon summation of respondent's
scores on the three included authoritarianism items and
computed in the manner described for computation of
four-level authoritarianism index score above, except
that only two levels of authoritarianism are defined in
this authoritarianism index score.

(0) - None answered or some, but not all, answered.
(1) - Score between 3 and 7 = Not authoritarian.
(2) - Score between 8 and 12 = Authoritarian.

NOTE: Question 3z was not included with the other
three authoritarianism items in this computation, since
it did not correlate positively with them.

PERSONAL CYNICISM INDEX SCORE (ABSOLUTE), 4 LEVELS
    (7a-7d):

   Index score based upon summation of respondent's
scores on the four personal cynicism items. Items summed,
and index score determined for each respondent, only if
all four items were answered. Zero value punched if
fewer than all four were answered. Index scores determined on basis of summation of the respondent's answers
to the four personal cynicism items, with the index
score assigned being dependent upon where that total
score fell within specified ranges of scores on the
four items, as follows:

(0) - None answered or some, but not all, answered.
(1) - Score between 4 and 6 = LOW personal cynicism.
(2) - Score between 7 and 10 = SLIGHT personal cynicism
(3) - Score between 11 and 13 = MODERATE personal
                                cynicism.
(4) - Score between 14 and 16 = HIGH personal cynicism.

   NOTE: All four items in the personal cynicism series
were included in the computation of the mean score, since
all correlated positively.

PERSONAL CYNICISM INDEX SCORE (ABSOLUTE), 2 LEVELS
    (Q. 7a-7d):

   Index score based upon summation of respondent's
scores on the four personal cynicism items and computed
in the manner described for computation of the four-level
personal cynicism index score above, except that only
two levels of personal cynicism are defined in this
personal cynicism index score.

(0) - None answered or some, but not all, answered.
(1) - Score between 4 and 10 = Not cynical.
(2) - Score between 11 and 16 = Cynical.

   NOTE: All four items in the personal cynicism series
were included in this computation, since all four
correlated positively.

FOOTNOTES TO ITEMS IN QUESTIONNAIRE

[1]J.Dudley McClain, Jr., "1972-73 Southern College Student Attitude Study." Questionnaire and Coding Outline, p. 1. Item written by researcher specifically for this study.

[2]Ibid.

[3]Ibid.

[4]Ibid.

[5]Modification of "Party Identification" question which originated with the 1952 Survey Research Center election study and also appeared in its election studies of 1956, 1960, and 1964. Also reported in: Angus Campbell, Philip E. Converse, Warren E. Miller and Donald E. Stokes, The American Voter (New York: John Wiley and Sons, Inc., 1960); Angus Campbell, Philip E. Converse, Warren E. Miller, and Donald E. Stokes, Elections and the Political Order (New York: John Wiley and Sons, Inc., 1966); Philip E. Converse, "The Nature of Belief Systems in Mass Publics,: in David Apter (ed.), Ideology and Discontent (New York: Free Press, 1964); Philip E. Converse, "The Concept of a Normal Vote," in Angus Campbell et al., (eds.), Elections and the Political Order; Gallup Opinion Index (Princeton, N. J.: Gallup International, Inc., November, 1967); John P. Robinson, Jerrold G. Rusk, and Kendra B. Head, Measures of Political Attitudes (Ann Arbor, Mich.: Survey Research Center, Institute for Social Research, The University of Michigan, 1968), p. 496. Various forms or modifications of this party identification item have appeared in a large number of other studies as well.

[6]This item is a modification of the "liberalism-conservatism" question which originated with the Gallup Opinion Index (Princeton, N. J.: Gallup International, Inc.).

[7]Modification of item #1 in the "Trust in Government (Cynicism) Scale," or "Attitude Toward Government" series, first used in the Survey Research Center's 1958 election study and later used in its 1964 and 1966 election studies. See John P. Robinson et al., Measures of Political Attitudes, p. 643, and fn. 16, pp. 655-58. This is also essentially the same question as one reported in the Appendix to the Report of the National Advisory Commission on Civil Disorders in 1966.

[8]Ibid.

[9]Ibid.

[10]Modification of item #1 in the "Trust in Government (Cynicism) Scale," or "Attitude Toward Government" series, note 7, above. Also used in modified form in the study of riots in Newark, reported in "Footnotes: Chaper Two" of Appendix K to Report of the National Advisory Commission on Civil Disorders (Washington, D.C.: U. S. Government Printing Office, 1968), p. 335. See John P. Robinson et al., Measures of Political Attitudes, p. 643.

[11]Ibid.

[12]One of the two basic response devices used in the 1972-73 Southern College Student Attitude Study was the standard four-part "agree-disagree" device designed to measure both direction and strength (on two levels) of feeling. Device is of the type which originated with Rensis Likert and was reported in "A Technique for the Measurement of Attitudes," Archives of Psychology (1932): 1-55.

[13]Question was suggested in letter from William A. Gamson to Gordon G. Henderson for inclusion in Henderson's 1971 study of Lubbock, Texas, citizen attitudes.

[14]Item originated with the Survey Research Center's
1948 election study as item #4 of its "Political
Efficacy" series and was also used in its 1956, 1964 and
1968 election studies. This item, and the other
"political efficacy" items to which reference is made
by notes 15 and 16 below, also appeared in Angus
Campbell et al., The Voter Decides, pp. 187-89, and in
Andrew F. Henry, "A Method of Classifying Non-scale
Response Patterns in a Guttman Scale," Public Opinion
Quarterly 16 (Spring 1952): 94-106. These "political
efficacy" items have been used in every major SRC election study since 1948 and in a number of other studies.

[15]Ibid., item #3.

[16]Ibid., item #2.

[17]Item originated as item #2 of the "Political
Efficacy Scale" devised by Angus Campbell et al., which
also incorporated the three "political efficacy" items
referenced in notes 14 through 16, above, and which
appeared in Angus Campbell et al., The Voter Decides,
pp. 187-89. See also John P. Robinson et al., Measures
of Political Attitudes, p. 460, fn. 4, pp. 635-36.

[18]This item on "Sense of Law-abidingness," which is
used in this study as a measure of one aspect of
"political obligation," along with the other nine items
which constitute questions 3(f) through 3(o) of this
questionnaire for the 1972-73 Southern College Student
Attitude Study, was first used by Gordon G. Henderson
in his 1970 study of citizen attitudes in Lubbock, Texas,
and originated with the author and others in a graduate
seminar under Dr. Henderson.

[19]Ibid.

[20]Ibid.

[21]Ibid.

[22]Ibid.

[23]Ibid.

[24] Ibid.

[25] Ibid.

[26] Ibid.

[27] Ibid.

[28] Item originated as item #2 of the twelve items
included in the first form of the "Conservatism Scale"
which initially appeared in Herbert McCloskey, "Conservatism and Personality," American Political Science
Review 52 (1958): 27–45. Item was also used by Angus
Campbell et al., in The American Voter, pp. 210–212. See
John P. Robinson et al., Measures of Political Attitudes,
p. 96. The "conservatism" measures used in this study
of college students also constitute a modification of
items two through five of the "People and Life Scale"
used in the 1958 Survey Research Center election study,
reported in Robinson et al., fn. 16, pp. 668–69.

[29] Item is a modification of item #3 of the McCloskey
"Conservatism Scale" referenced in note 28 above. Item
was also used by Campbell et al. in The American Voter
in 1960 and by David R. Matthews and James W. Prothro in
Negroes and the New Southern Politics (New York:
Harcourt, Brace and World, 1966), p. 526. See John P.
Robinson et al., Measures of Political Attitudes (Ann
Arbor, Mich.: Survey Research Center, 1968), p. 96.

[30] Ibid., item #4 of McCloskey "Conservatism Scale."

[31] Item was question #5 of the McCloskey "Conservatism
Scale" and was used by Matthews and Prothro in Negroes
and the New Southern Politics, all referenced in notes
28 through 30, above. See John P. Robinson et al.,
Measures of Political Attitudes, p. 96.

[32] Ibid, item #6 of McCloskey "Conservatism Scale."

[33] Item originated as question #65 of the report by
Streuning and Efron on their study of opinions of former
mental patients about their work, included in scoring
the factor of "Alienation from a Rejecting Environment"

and reported in "The Dimensional Structure of Opinions about Work and the Social Context," Journal of Counseling Psychology 12 (Fall 1965): 317.

[34]Ibid., item #69, Streuning and Efron "alienation" series.

[35]Item is a modification of question #3 of the "Anomia Scale" reported by L. Srole in "Social Integration and Certain Corollaries," American Sociological Review 21 (1956): 709-16.

[36]Streuning and Efron, notes 33 and 34 above, question #23.

[37]Item was used in this 1972-73 Southern College Student Attitude Study questionnaire, along with the three Streuning and Efron "alienation" items referenced in notes 33, 34 and 36, and the item referenced in note 35, above, as a series intended to measure what has for the purposes of this study of student attitudes been designated as one's "Sense of Personal Alienation."

[38]Modification of items which originated as items #13 and #20 of the "Initial Politico-economic Conservatism Scale (Form 60)" used by T. W. Adorno and others as one of the "liberal" items among their series of questions seeking to assess the "Authoritarian Personality." See T. W. Adorno, Else Frankel-Brunswick, Daniel J. Levinson, and R. Nevitt Sanford, The Authoritarian Personality (New York: Harper and Row, 1950). Item also appeared as question #1 of the 1956 Survey Research Center post-election study. See John P. Robinson et al., Measure of Political Attitudes, p. 664. This item and the other three "authoritarianism" items which are referenced in notes 39 through 41, below, also appeared in Angus Campbell et al., The American Voter, p. 512.

[39]Ibid., item #59 of the Adorno "Fascism (F) Scale: Form 78," item #6 of the Adorno "F-Scale Clusters: Forms 45 and 40," p. 255, and item #3 of SRC series, fn. 38.

⁴⁰Ibid. Modified version of item #60 of the Adorno "Fascism (F) Scale: Form 60," p. 248, item #13 of the Adorno "F-Scale Clusters: Forms 45 and 40," p. 255, and item #5 of the Survey Research Center series, all referenced in notes 38 and 39, above.

⁴¹Item originated as question #6 of the "Authoritarianism Items" used in the 1956 Survey Research Center post-election study. See Angus Campbell et al., The American Voter, p. 512 fn., and John P. Robinson et al., Measures of Political Attitudes, p. 665.

⁴²The "feeling thermometer" device for measuring both the direction and intensity of feeling has been used in many previous studies. It originated with the Center for Political Studies of the University of Michigan, as best the author can determine.

⁴³McClain, 1972-73 Southern College Student Attitude Study. The items comprising the question series on "Political Interest Groups" which appear as questions 4(a) through 4(t) of this questionnaire for the 1972-73 Southern College Student Attitude Study were written by the researcher specifically for this study.

⁴⁴Ibid. The items comprising the question series on "Political Figures" which appear as questions 5(a) through 5(x) of this 1972-73 Southern College Student Attitude Study were written by the researcher specifically for this study.

⁴⁵Ibid. The items comprising the question series on "Feelings Toward Labor Unions for Selected Groups" which appear as questions 6(a) through 6(r) of this 1972-73 Southern College Student Attitude Study were written by the researcher specifically for this study.

⁴⁶Item originally appeared as question #1 of the "Personal Competence," or "Personal Cynicism," set in the "personality variable" series in the 1956 post-election study by the Survey Research Center. See John P. Robinson et al., Measures of Political Attitudes, pp. 655-58.

[47]Ibid., item #5.

[48]Ibid., item #11.

[49]Ibid., item #12.

[50]McClain, 1972-73 Southern College Student Attitude Study questionnaire. The items comprising the question series on "Attitudes Toward Labor Policy" which appear as questions 8(a) through 8(cc) of the 1972-73 Southern College Student Attitude Study questionnaire were derived from several sources, as the following footnotes indicate. This item and the others in that series which inquire whether specified groups of workers "should have the right to be in a labor union" and which inquire whether specified groups of workers "should have the right to strike" were all written by the researcher specifically for this study. The first group includes questions 8(a), 8(b), 8(d), 8(e), 8(g), 8(h), 8(i), 8(k) and 8(1). The latter group includes questions 8(n), 8(o), 8(q), 8(r), 8(t), 8(u), 8(w), 8(x) and 8(bb).

[51]Ibid.

[52]Item originated as question #12(1) of the series on "Issue Familiarity" in Angus Campbell et al., The American Voter, pp. 171-76. See John P. Robinson et al., Measures of Political Attitudes, p. 422.

[53]McClain, note 50, above.

[54]Ibid.

[55]Item originated as one of the "liberal" questions used on both the second (Form 60) and third (Form 40-45) forms of the "Political Economic Conservatism Scale," or PEC Scale," used by Adorno and others and reported in T. W. Adorno et al., The Authoritarian Personality. See John P. Robinson et al., Measures of Political Attitudes, p. 111-12.

[56]McClain, note 50, above.

[57]Ibid.

[58]Ibid.

[59]Item originated as one of the questions in the "Ideological Military-Pacificism (IMP) Scale" used in Lawrence A. Dombrose and Daniel J. Levinson, "Ideological 'Militancy' and 'Pacificism' in Democratic Individuals," Journal of Social Psychology 32 (1950): 101-113. See John P. Robinson et al., Measures of Political Attitudes, p. 373.

[60]McClain, note 50, above.

[61]Ibid.

[62]Item originated as question #6 of the "Labor Union Series" which comprised Part III of the measures of "Attitudes Toward Government, Large Companies and Labor Unions" reported in The Initiators (Princeton, N. J.: Opinion Research Corporation, 1960), pp. T-4 to T-7. See John P. Robinson et al., Measures of Political Attitudes, p. 197.

[63]McClain, note 50, above.

[64]Ibid.

[65]The Initiators, note 62 above, question #1.

[66]McClain, note 50, above.

[67]Ibid.

[68]Item originated as question #15 of series on "Understanding the Union Member" in study by W. Uphoff and M. Dunnette and was reported in the "IRC Union Attitude Scale" in John P. Robinson et al., Measures of Occupational Attitudes, p. 288.

[69]McClain, note 50, above.

[70]Ibid.

[71]Uphoff and Dunnette, note 68, above. Original question #20.

[72]McClain, note 50, above.

[73]Ibid.

[74]Item originated as question #84 of G. Hartman's "Liberalism-Conservatism Scale," which was reported in "The Differential Validity of Items in a Liberalism-Conservatism Test," Journal of Social Psychology 9 (1938): 67-78.

[75]Ibid., original question #100.

[76]Dombrose and Levinson, "IMP Scale," note 59, above.

[77]McClain, note 50, above.

[78]Hartman, "Liberalism-Conservatism Scale, note 74, above, original question #46.

[79]McClain, 1972-73 Southern College Student Attitude Study. This question on preferences for the Democratic Party nomination for the presidency in 1972 was written by the researcher specifically for this study. The question as it appears (in the past tense) in this post-election version of the questionnaire, was phrased for consideration by the two groups of students who were interviewed after the election. The question, as it initially appeared (in the present tense) in the pre-election version of the questionnaire, was phrased as follows for consideration by the two groups of students who were interviewed prior to the election:

"A large number of people at one time or another announced that they would seek the Democratic Party nomination for the Presidency in the 1972 election, or are considered prospects even though they may not have made any formal announcement that they are candidates for the nomination. The list has included (in alphabetical order): Shirley Chisholm, Vance Hartke, Hubert Humphrey, Henry Jackson, Edward Kennedy, John Lindsay, Eugene McCarthy, George McGovern, Lester Maddox,

Wilbur Mills, Edmund Muskie, Terry Sanford, George
Wallace, and Sam Yorty. If all of these were still
in the running, which one would you prefer to see get
the Democratic Party nomination?"

[80]Ibid. This question on preferences in a series
of hypothetical two-way races, each between a specified
Democratic Party nominee and Nixon as the Republican
Party nominee, each not involving George Wallace running
as a third-party candidate, was written by the researcher
specifically for this study. The question, as it
appears (in the past tense) in this post-election
version of the questionnaire, was phrased for consideration by the two groups of students who were interviewed
after the election. The question, as it initially
appeared (in the present tense) in the pre-election
version of the questionnaire, was phrased as follows
for consideration by the two groups of students who were
interviewed prior to the election:

"Suppose the election for President took place today.
Below we have listed some of the conceivable pairings
of Democratic Party nominees against the likely
Republican Party nominee in hypothetical two-way races.
For each separate pairing, please check the name of the
person you would prefer to see elected President in
1972."

[81]Ibid. This question on preferences in a series of
hypothetical three-way races for the presidency, each
involving a specified Democratic Party nominee, Nixon
as the Republican Party nominee, and George Wallace as
a third-party candidate, was written by the researcher
specifically for this study. The question, as it
appears (in the past tense) in this post-election
version of the questionnaire, was phrased for consideration by the two groups of students who were interviewed
after the election. The question, as it initially
appeared (in the present tense) in the pre-election
version of the questionnaire, was phrased as follows
for consideration by the two groups of students who
were interviewed prior to the election:

"Next, suppose the race for the Presidency were a

three-way race involving Richard Nixon as the Republican
candidate, George Wallace as a third-party candidate,
and the individual listed below in each instance as the
Democratic candidate. For each of the following conceivable three-way races, check the one of the three
candidates you would prefer."

[82]Ibid. Item written specifically for this study.

[83]This question on marital status is a slightly
modified version of a standard item which has been used
in a substantial number of survey studies. It appears,
for example, in the codebook of the 1972 election study
by the Center for Political Studies of the University of
Michigan.

[84]Coding scheme used for question on state of
student's "home town," or "place of permanent residence,"
was that which originated with the Survey Research Center
and which has been used by it in many studies.

[85]McClain, note 82, above.

[86]Ibid.

[87]Ibid.

[88]Ibid.

[89]Ibid.

[90]Ibid.

[91]The coding categories used for this question
on student's anticipated future occupational area
following graduation were adapted directly from the
major occupational division "headings" from the
"occupations" coding scheme used by the Survey Research
Center.

[92]Ibid.

[93]McClain, note 82, above.

[94]Ibid.

95Ibid.

96Ibid.

97Ibid.

98This question closely resembles a standard item
on frequency of church attendance. A very similar item
appears, for example, in the 1972 election study of the
Center for Political Studies of the University of
Michigan.

99This question constitutes a modification of a
standard item on perceived social class. It appears,
for instance, in the 1972 election study by the Center
for Political Studies of the University of Michigan.

100McClain, note 82, above.

101This question was written by the researcher
specifically for this study of college students and
attempts to take into account their unique circumstances.
It bears some resemblance to a similar standard and often
used item.

102McClain, note 82, above.

103This question is patterned after one used by
Gordon G. Henderson in a 1963 survey he conducted in
Mississippi.

104This question, as was the case with question #34,
is patterned after one used by Gordon Henderson in his
1963 survey in Mississippi.

105Modification of standard Survey Research Center
"Party Identification" question. See note 5, above.

III
PROFILES OF
BLACK COLLEGE STUDENTS

EXPLANATION OF NUMBERING OF TABLES

The tables which comprise the remainder of this volume are numbered and labeled according to the same scheme and follow the same format as those used in the other volumes of this Southern College Student Profiles series. The labels for the tables are abbreviations of the questions in the survey instrument from which the data in each table were obtained. The tables in this volume can be compared directly to similar data tables in the other volumes in this series bearing the same number and label as the tables in this volume.

Thus, the tables in every volume in the series have been numbered and labeled in such a way that like data for the respective student group which is the subject of each volume in the series can be compared directly to like data for each of the other groups.

The number given each table is composed of a Roman numeral, which indicates the interview group (of the four groups of interviews), followed by an Arabic numeral and, where appropriate, a letter in parentheses, which correspond to the number of the question in the survey instrument for which the table presents the response data.

Thus, a table numbered "II-3(f)" would present data from the responses of interview Group II to question number 3(f), and a table numbered "III-3(f)" would present data from the responses of interview Group III to question number 3(f). The tables for similar data for interview groups I and IV would be numbered I-3(f) and IV-3(f), respectively.

This volume on black students is based upon data from interview groups II and III, since very few black students were included in either group I or group IV. Thus, this volume only includes tables for groups II and III, and the tables which follow in this section are numbered accordingly. Each table for group II in this volume can, however, be compared directly to the like table for group II in each of the other volumes in the series. So, too, can each table for group III in this volume be compared directly to the like table for Group III in each of the other volumes in the series.

81

POLITICAL PARTICIPATION
AND ORIENTATION

POLYGALACT[...]
[...]

Q. 1(a): Did R vote in 1968? [1]

TABLE II-1(a): GROUP II (Fall, 1972).

Category Label	n	%
0. No response	12	1.3
1. No	236	25.8
2. Yes	89	9.7
3. Too young	577	63.1
TOTAL	914	100.0

TABLE III-1(a): GROUP III (Spring, 1973).

Category Label	n	%
0. No response	22	2.2
1. No	201	20.4
2. Yes	181	18.4
3. Too young	580	58.9
TOTAL	984	100.0

Q. 1(b).   Is R registered to vote? [2]

TABLE II-1(b): GROUP II (Fall, 1972).

Category Label	n	%
0. No response	7	0.8
1. No	258	28.2
2. Yes	649	71.0
TOTAL	914	100.0

TABLE III-1(b): GROUP III (Spring, 1973).

Category Label	n	%
0. No response	10	1.0
1. No	176	17.9
2. Yes	798	81.1
TOTAL	984	100.0

Q. 1(c). Has R been active in campaign? [3]

TABLE II-1(c): GROUP II (Fall, 1972).

Category Label	n	%
0. No response	4	0.4
1. No	630	68.9
2. Yes	280	30.6
TOTAL	914	100.0

TABLE III-1(c): GROUP III (Spring, 1973).

Category Label	n	%
0. No response	14	1.4
1. No	667	67.8
2. Yes	303	30.8
TOTAL	984	100.0

Q. 1(d).   Is R member of any political party? [4]

TABLE II-1(d): GROUP II (Fall, 1972).

Category Label	n	%
0. No response	14	1.5
1. No	589	64.4
2. Yes	311	34.0
TOTAL	914	100.0

TABLE III-1(d): GROUP III (Spring, 1973).

Category Label	n	%
0. No response	20	2.0
1. No	637	64.7
2. Yes	327	33.2
TOTAL	984	100.0

Participation Index Score (Absolute), 4 levels.
(See Coding Outline, page 22).

TABLE II-1(b)-1(d): GROUP II (Fall, 1972).

Category Label	n	%
0. No response	18	2.0
1. None	196	21.4
2. Slight	288	31.5
3. Moderate	294	32.2
4. High	118	12.9
TOTAL	914	100.0

Mean	2.373	Std. err.	0.032
Mode	3.000	Std. dev.	0.967
Kurtosis	-0.991	Skewness	0.073
Median	2.375	Variance	0.936

Range for computation of statistics: 1 through 4.

TABLE III-1(b)-1(d): GROUP III (Spring, 1973).

Category Label	n	%
0. No response	24	2.4
1. None	126	12.8
2. Slight	397	40.3
3. Moderate	296	30.1
4. High	141	14.3
TOTAL	984	100.0

Mean	2.471	Std. err.	0.029
Mode	2.000	Std. dev.	0.898
Kurtosis	-0.749	Skewness	0.152
Median	2.392	Variance	0.806

Range for computation of statistics: 1 through 4.

Q. 1(e). Pro-Republican party identification.[5]

TABLE II-1(e): GROUP II (Fall, 1972).

Category Label	n	%
0. No response	18	2.0
1. Strong Democrat	294	32.2
2. Not very strong Dem.	185	20.2
3. Independent lean. Dem.	252	27.6
4. Independent	107	11.7
5. Independent lean. Repub.	13	1.4
6. Not very strong Repub.	9	1.0
7. Strong Republican	10	1.1
8. American Party	4	0.4
9. Other party	22	2.4
TOTAL	914	100.0

Mean	2.341	Std. err.	0.043
Mode	1.000	Std. dev.	1.262
Kurtosis	0.987	Skewness	0.882
Median	2.262	Variance	1.592

Range for computation of statistics: 1 through 7.

TABLE III-1(e): GROUP III (Spring, 1973).

Category Label	n	%
0. No response	28	2.8
1. Strong Democrat	270	27.4
2. Not very strong Dem.	196	19.9
3. Independent lean. Dem.	332	33.7
4. Independent	118	12.0
5. Independent lean. Repub.	7	0.7
6. Not very strong Repub.	7	0.7
7. Strong Republican	2	0.2
8. American Party	4	0.4
9. Other party	20	2.0
TOTAL	984	100.0

Mean	2.383	Std. err.	0.037
Mode	3.000	Std. dev.	1.117
Kurtosis	-0.049	Skewness	0.389
Median	2.500	Variance	1.248

Range for computation of statistics: 1 through 7.

POLITICAL ORIENTATION

1(e). Pro-Democratic Party Identification.[5]

TABLE II-1(e): GROUP II (Fall, 1972).

Category Label	n	%
0. No response	18	2.0
1. Strong Republican	10	1.1
2. Not very strong Repub.	9	1.0
3. Independent lean. Repub.	13	1.4
4. Independent	107	11.7
5. Independent lean. Dem.	252	27.6
6. Not very strong Dem.	185	20.2
7. Strong Democrat	294	32.2
8. American Party	4	0.4
9. Other party	22	2.4
TOTAL	914	100.0

Mean	5.659	Std. err.	0.043
Mode	7.000	Std. dev.	1.262
Kurtosis	0.987	Skewness	-0.882
Median	5.738	Variance	1.592

Range for computation of statistics: 1 through 7.

TABLE III-1(e): GROUP III (Spring, 1973).

Category Label	n	%
0. No response	28	2.8
1. Strong Repub.	2	0.2
2. Not very strong Repub.	7	0.7
3. Independent lean. Repub.	7	0.7
4. Independent	118	12.0
5. Independent lean. Dem.	332	33.7
6. Not very strong Dem.	196	19.9
7. Strong Democrat	270	27.4
8. American Party	4	0.4
9. Other party	20	2.0
TOTAL	984	100.0

Mean	5.617	Std. err.	0.037
Mode	5.000	Std. dev.	1.117
Kurtosis	-0.049	Skewness	-0.389
Median	5.500	Variance	1.248

Range for computation of statistics: 1 through 7.

Q. 1(f). Perception of Liberalism, Conservatism.[6]

TABLE II-1(f): GROUP II (Fall, 1972).

Category Label	n	%
0. No response	18	2.0
1. Conservative	209	22.9
2. Liberal	640	70.0
3. Other	47	5.1
TOTAL	914	100.0

TABLE III-1(f): GROUP III (Spring, 1973).

Category Label	n	%
0. No response	23	2.3
1. Conservative	219	22.3
2. Liberal	674	68.5
3. Other	68	6.9
TOTAL	984	100.0

POLITICAL ATTITUDES
AND SUPPORT FOR
THE POLITICAL SYSTEM

Q. 2(a).   Trust in government in Washington. [7]

TABLE II-2(a):   GROUP II (Fall, 1972).

Category Label	n	%
0. No response	7	0.8
1. Almost never	178	19.5
2. Some of time	482	52.7
3. Most of time	206	22.5
4. Almost always	41	4.5
TOTAL	914	100.0

Mean	2.105	Std. err.	0.026
Mode	2.000	Std. dev.	0.787
Kurtosis	0.033	Skewness	0.271
Median	2.064	Variance	0.620

Range for computation of statistics: 1 through 4.

TABLE III-2(a):   GROUP III (Spring, 1973).

Category Label	n	%
0. No response	6	0.6
1. Almost never	225	22.9
2. Some of time	567	57.6
3. Most of time	165	16.8
4. Almost always	21	2.1
TOTAL	984	100.0

Mean	1.970	Std. err.	0.023
Mode	2.000	Std. dev.	0.711
Kurtosis	0.310	Skewness	0.298
Median	1.960	Variance	0.506

Range for computation of statistics: 1 through 4.

Q. 2(b). Trust in state government. [8]

TABLE II-2(b): GROUP II (Fall, 1972).

Category Label	n	%
0. No response	6	0.7
1. Almost never	293	32.1
2. Some of time	436	47.7
3. Most of time	150	16.4
4. Almost always	29	3.2
TOTAL	914	100.0

Mean	1.894	Std. err.	0.026
Mode	2.000	Std. dev.	0.792
Kurtosis	-0.051	Skewness	0.495
Median	1.862	Variance	0.627

Range for computation of statistics: 1 through 4.

TABLE III-2(b): GROUP III (Spring, 1973).

Category Label	n	%
0. No response	7	0.7
1. Almost never	234	23.8
2. Some of time	545	55.4
3. Most of time	173	17.6
4. Almost always	25	2.5
TOTAL	984	100.0

Mean	1.975	Std. err.	0.024
Mode	2.000	Std. dev.	0.737
Kurtosis	0.200	Skewness	0.314
Median	1.961	Variance	0.544

Range for computation of statistics: 1 through 4.

Q. 2(c). Trust in city government. [9]

TABLE II-2(c): GROUP II (Fall, 1972).

Category Label		n	%
0.	No response	7	0.8
1.	Almost never	282	30.9
2.	Some of time	431	47.2
3.	Most of time	163	17.8
4.	Almost always	31	3.4
TOTAL		914	100.0

Mean	1.922	Std. err.	0.027
Mode	2.000	Std. dev.	0.805
Kurtosis	−0.137	Skewness	0.444
Median	1.890	Variance	0.648

Range for computation of statistics: 1 through 4.

TABLE III-2(c): GROUP III (Spring, 1973).

Category Label		n	%
0.	No response	6	0.6
1.	Almost never	325	33.0
2.	Some of time	479	48.7
3.	Most of time	148	15.0
4.	Almost always	26	2.6
TOTAL		984	100.0

Mean	1.861	Std. err.	0.025
Mode	2.000	Std. dev.	0.769
Kurtosis	0.031	Skewness	0.511
Median	1.836	Variance	0.592

Range for computation of statistics: 1 through 4.

Q. 2(d). Executive officer trusts most. [10]

TABLE II-2(d): GROUP II (Fall, 1972).

Category Label	n	%
0. No response	47	5.1
1. President	348	38.1
2. Governor	194	21.2
3. Mayor	325	35.6
TOTAL	914	100.0

TABLE III-2(d): GROUP III (Spring, 1973).

Category Label	n	%
0. No response	78	7.9
1. President	222	22.6
2. Governor	392	39.8
3. Mayor	292	29.7
TOTAL	984	100.0

Q. 2(e).   Executive officer trusts least. [11]

TABLE II-2(e):   GROUP II (Fall, 1972).

Category Label	n	%
0. No response	38	4.2
1. President	284	31.1
2. Governor	331	36.2
3. Mayor	261	28.6
TOTAL	914	100.0

TABLE III-2(e):   GROUP III (Spring, 1973).

Category Label	n	%
0. No response	47	4.8
1. President	519	52.7
2. Governor	105	10.7
3. Mayor	313	31.8
TOTAL	984	100.0

Q. 3(a). Think of government in Washington as enemy.[13]

TABLE II-3(a): GROUP II (Fall, 1972).

Category Label	n	%
0. No response	5	0.5
1. Agree a lot	171	18.7
2. Agree a little	284	31.1
3. Disagree a little	286	31.3
4. Disagree a lot	168	18.4
TOTAL	914	100.0

Mean	2.482	Std. err.	0.033
Mode	3.000	Std. dev.	1.013
Kurtosis	-0.976	Skewness	-0.041
Median	2.489	Variance	1.025

Range for computation of statistics: 1 through 4.

TABLE III-3(a): GROUP III (Spring, 1973).

Category Label	n	%
0. No response	4	0.4
1. Agree a lot	255	25.9
2. Agree a little	317	32.2
3. Disagree a little	274	27.8
4. Disagree a lot	134	13.6
TOTAL	984	100.0

Mean	2.284	Std. err.	0.032
Mode	2.000	Std. dev.	1.010
Kurtosis	-1.004	Skewness	0.182
Median	2.235	Variance	1.019

Range for computation of statistics: 1 through 4.

Trust Index Score (Absolute), 4 levels.
(See Coding Outline, page 30).

TABLE II-2(a)-3(a): GROUP II (Fall, 1972).

Category Label	n	%
0. No response	14	1.5
1. Low	137	15.0
2. Slight	488	53.4
3. Moderate	257	28.1
4. High	18	2.0
TOTAL	914	100.0

Mean	2.173	Std. err.	0.023
Mode	2.000	Std. dev.	0.699
Kurtosis	−0.291	Skewness	0.101
Median	2.141	Variance	0.488

Range for computation of statistics: 1 through 4.

TABLE III-2(a)-3(a): GROUP III (Spring, 1973).

Category Label	n	%
0. No response	13	1.3
1. Low	170	17.3
2. Slight	567	57.6
3. Moderate	223	22.7
4. High	11	1.1
TOTAL	984	100.0

Mean	2.077	Std. err.	0.021
Mode	2.000	Std. dev.	0.667
Kurtosis	−0.178	Skewness	0.141
Median	2.056	Variance	0.445

Range for computation of statistics: 1 through 4.

Trust Index Score (Absolute), 2 levels.
(See Coding Outline, page 30).

TABLE II-2(a)-3(a): GROUP II (Fall, 1972).

Category Label	n	%
0. No response	14	1.5
1. Not trusting	625	68.4
2. Trusting	275	30.1
TOTAL	914	100.0

Mean	1.306	Std. err.	0.015
Mode	1.000	Std. dev.	0.461
Kurtosis	-1.289	Skewness	0.844
Median	1.220	Variance	0.212

Range for computation of statistics: 1 through 2.

TABLE III-2(a)-3(a): GROUP III (Spring, 1973).

Category Label	n	%
0. No response	13	1.3
1. Not trusting	737	74.9
2. Trusting	234	23.8
TOTAL	984	100.0

Mean	1.241	Std. err.	0.014
Mode	1.000	Std. dev.	0.428
Kurtosis	-0.535	Skewness	1.211
Median	1.159	Variance	0.183

Range for computation of statistics: 1 through 2.

Trust Index Score (Relative), 4 levels.
(See Coding Outline, page 23).

TABLE II-2(a)-3(a): GROUP II (Fall, 1972).

Category Label	n	%
0. No response	14	1.5
1. Low	460	50.3
2. Slight	299	32.7
3. Moderate	71	7.8
4. High	70	7.7
TOTAL	914	100.0

Mean	1.723	Std. err.	0.030
Mode	1.000	Std. dev.	0.909
Kurtosis	0.586	Skewness	1.195
Median	1.478	Variance	0.825

Range for computation of statistics: 1 through 4.

TABLE III-2(a)-3(a): GROUP III (Spring, 1973).

Category Label	n	%
0. No response	13	1.3
1. Low	522	53.0
2. Slight	344	35.0
3. Moderate	56	5.7
4. High	49	5.0
TOTAL	984	100.0

Mean	1.621	Std. err.	0.026
Mode	1.000	Std. dev.	0.809
Kurtosis	1.473	Skewness	1.365
Median	1.430	Variance	0.654

Range for computation of statistics: 1 through 4.

Trust Index Score (Relative), 2 levels.
(See Coding Outline, page 23).

TABLE II-2(a)-3(a): GROUP II (Fall, 1972).

Category Label	n	%
0. No response	14	1.5
1. Not trusting	625	68.4
2. Trusting	275	30.1
TOTAL	914	100.0

Mean	1.306	Std. err.	0.015
Mode	1.000	Std. dev.	0.461
Kurtosis	-1.289	Skewness	0.844
Median	1.220	Variance	0.212

Range for computation of statistics: 1 through 2.

TABLE III-2(a)-3(a): GROUP III (Spring, 1973).

Category Label	n	%
0. No response	13	1.3
1. Not trusting	737	74.9
2. Trusting	234	23.8
TOTAL	984	100.0

Mean	1.241	Std. err.	0.014
Mode	1.000	Std. dev.	0.428
Kurtosis	-0.535	Skewness	1.211
Median	1.159	Variance	0.183

Range for computation of statistics: 1 through 2.

Q. 3(b). Public officials don't care what think.[14]

TABLE II-3(b): GROUP II (Fall, 1972).

Category Label	n	%
0. No response	6	0.7
1. Agree a lot	350	38.3
2. Agree a little	294	32.2
3. Disagree a little	195	21.3
4. Disagree a lot	69	7.5
TOTAL	914	100.0

Mean	1.968	Std. err.	0.032
Mode	1.000	Std. dev.	0.962
Kurtosis	-0.701	Skewness	0.529
Median	1.844	Variance	0.925

Range for computation of statistics: 1 through 4.

TABLE III-3(b): GROUP III (Spring, 1973).

Category Label	n	%
0. No response	5	0.5
1. Agree a lot	394	40.0
2. Agree a little	333	33.8
3. Disagree a little	178	18.1
4. Disagree a lot	74	7.5
TOTAL	984	100.0

Mean	1.921	Std. err.	0.030
Mode	1.000	Std. dev.	0.947
Kurtosis	-0.502	Skewness	0.654
Median	1.779	Variance	0.897

Range for computation of statistics: 1 through 4.

Q. 3(c). Politics so complicated can't understand.[15]

TABLE II-3(c): GROUP II (Fall, 1972).

Category Label	n	%
0. No response	10	1.1
1. Agree a lot	292	31.9
2. Agree a little	310	33.9
3. Disagree a little	173	18.9
4. Disagree a lot	129	14.1
TOTAL	914	100.0

Mean	2.130	Std. err.	0.035
Mode	2.000	Std. dev.	1.049
Kurtosis	-0.870	Skewness	0.415
Median	2.000	Variance	1.101

Range for computation of statistics: 1 through 4.

TABLE III-3(b): GROUP III (Spring, 1973).

Category Label	n	%
0. No response	11	1.1
1. Agree a lot	331	33.6
2. Agree a little	309	31.4
3. Disagree a little	162	16.5
4. Disagree a lot	171	17.4
TOTAL	984	100.0

Mean	2.153	Std. err.	0.035
Mode	1.000	Std. dev.	1.104
Kurtosis	-1.017	Skewness	0.421
Median	1.985	Variance	1.219

Range for computation of statistics: 1 through 4.

Q. 3(d). Voting is only way can have a say.[16]

TABLE II-3(d): GROUP II (Fall, 1972).

Category Label	n	%
0. No response	13	1.4
1. Agree a lot	431	47.2
2. Agree a little	178	19.5
3. Disagree a little	137	15.0
4. Disagree a lot	155	17.0
TOTAL	914	100.0

Mean	1.989	Std. err.	0.039
Mode	1.000	Std. dev.	1.165
Kurtosis	-1.044	Skewness	0.611
Median	1.573	Variance	1.358

Range for computation of statistics: 1 through 4.

TABLE III-3(d): GROUP III (Spring, 1973).

Category Label	n	%
0. No response	8	0.8
1. Agree a lot	397	40.3
2. Agree a little	222	22.6
3. Disagree a little	169	17.2
4. Disagree a lot	188	19.1
TOTAL	984	100.0

Mean	2.134	Std. err.	0.037
Mode	1.000	Std. dev.	1.164
Kurtosis	-1.230	Skewness	0.434
Median	1.892	Variance	1.355

Range for computation of statistics: 1 through 4.

Q. 3(e). Way people vote decides things.[17]

TABLE II-3(e): GROUP II (Fall, 1972).

Category Label	n	%
0. No response	12	1.3
1. Agree a lot	303	33.2
2. Agree a little	191	20.9
3. Disagree a little	163	17.8
4. Disagree a lot	245	26.8
TOTAL	914	100.0

Mean	2.357	Std. err.	0.041
Mode	1.000	Std. dev.	1.228
Kurtosis	-1.454	Skewness	0.123
Median	2.243	Variance	1.509

Range for computation of statistics: 1 through 4.

TABLE III-3(e): GROUP III (Spring, 1973).

Category Label	n	%
0. No response	8	0.8
1. Agree a lot	228	23.2
2. Agree a little	202	20.5
3. Disagree a little	227	23.1
4. Disagree a lot	319	32.4
TOTAL	984	100.0

Mean	2.631	Std. err.	0.038
Mode	4.000	Std. dev.	1.181
Kurtosis	-1.351	Skewness	-0.220
Median	2.738	Variance	1.395

Range for computation of statistics: 1 through 4.

Efficacy Index Score (Absolute), 4 levels.
(See Coding Outline, page 31),

TABLE II-3(b)-3(e): GROUP II (Fall, 1972).

Category Label	n	%
0. No response	22	2.4
1. Low	218	23.9
2. Slight	457	50.0
3. Moderate	191	20.9
4. High	26	2.8
TOTAL	914	100.0

Mean	2.028	Std. err.	0.025
Mode	2.000	Std. dev.	0.758
Kurtosis	-0.260	Skewness	0.355
Median	1.999	Variance	0.575

Range for computation of statistics: 1 through 4.

TABLE III-3(b)-3(e): GROUP III (Spring, 1973).

Category Label	n	%
0. No response	20	2.0
1. Low	220	22.4
2. Slight	482	49.0
3. Moderate	239	24.3
4. High	23	2.3
TOTAL	984	100.0

Mean	2.067	Std. err.	0.024
Mode	2.000	Std. dev.	0.753
Kurtosis	-0.463	Skewness	0.224
Median	2.044	Variance	0.568

Range for computation of statistics: 1 through 4.

Efficacy Index Score (Absolute), 2 levels.
(See Coding Outline, page 31).

TABLE II-3(b)-3(e): GROUP II (Fall, 1972).

Category Label	n	%
0. No response	22	2.4
1. Not efficacious	675	73.9
2. Efficacious	217	23.7
TOTAL	914	100.0

Mean	1.243	Std. err.	0.014
Mode	1.000	Std. dev.	0.429
Kurtosis	-0.571	Skewness	1.196
Median	1.161	Variance	0.184

Range for computation of statistics: 1 through 2.

TABLE III-3(b)-3(e): GROUP III (Spring, 1973).

Category Label	n	%
0. No response	20	2.0
1. Not efficacious	702	71.3
2. Efficacious	262	26.6
TOTAL	984	100.0

Mean	1.272	Std. err.	0.014
Mode	1.000	Std. dev.	0.445
Kurtosis	-0.950	Skewness	1.025
Median	1.187	Variance	0.198

Range for computation of statistics: 1 through 2.

Efficacy Index Score (Relative), 4 levels.
(See Coding Outline, page 24).

TABLE II-3(b)-3(e): GROUP II (Fall, 1972).

Category Label	n	%
0. No response	22	2.4
1. Low	367	40.2
2. Slight	308	33.7
3. Moderate	155	17.0
4. High	62	6.8
TOTAL	914	100.0

Mean	1.901	Std. err.	0.031
Mode	1.000	Std. dev.	0.924
Kurtosis	-0.432	Skewness	0.725
Median	1.756	Variance	0.854

Range for computation of statistics: 1 through 4.

TABLE III-3(b)-3(e): GROUP III (Spring, 1973).

Category Label	n	%
0. No response	20	2.0
1. Low	362	36.8
2. Slight	340	34.6
3. Moderate	206	20.9
4. High	56	5.7
TOTAL	984	100.0

Mean	1.954	Std. err.	0.029
Mode	1.000	Std. dev.	0.906
Kurtosis	-0.643	Skewness	0.559
Median	1.853	Variance	0.820

Range for computation of statistics: 1 through 4.

Efficacy Index Score (Relative), 2 levels.
(See Coding Outline, page 24).

TABLE II-3(b)-3(e): GROUP II (Fall, 1972).

Category Label	n	%
0. No response	22	2.4
1. Not efficacious	675	73.9
2. Efficacious	217	23.7
TOTAL	914	100.0

Mean	1.243	Std. err.	0.014
Mode	1.000	Std. dev.	0.429
Kurtosis	-0.571	Skewness	1.196
Median	1.161	Variance	0.184

Range for computation of statistics: 1 through 2.

TABLE III-3(b)-3(e): GROUP III (Spring, 1973).

Category Label	n	%
0. No response	20	2.0
1. Not efficacious	702	71.3
2. Efficacious	262	26.6
TOTAL	984	100.0

Mean	1.272	Std. err.	0.014
Mode	1.000	Std. dev.	0.445
Kurtosis	-0.950	Skewness	1.025
Median	1.187	Variance	0.198

Range for computation of statistics: 1 through 2.

Q. 3(f). No one excused for breaking the law. [18]

TABLE II-3(f): GROUP II (Fall, 1972).

Category Label	n	%
0. No response	20	2.2
1. Disagree a lot	260	28.4
2. Disagree a little	281	30.7
3. Agree a little	154	16.8
4. Agree a lot	199	21.8
TOTAL	914	100.0

Mean	2.276	Std. err.	0.038
Mode	2.000	Std. dev.	1.156
Kurtosis	-1.144	Skewness	0.211
Median	2.130	Variance	1.337

Range for computation of statistics: 1 through 4.

TABLE III-3(f): GROUP III (Spring, 1973).

Category Label	n	%
0. No response	20	2.0
1. Disagree a lot	305	31.0
2. Disagree a little	330	33.5
3. Agree a little	144	14.6
4. Agree a lot	185	18.8
TOTAL	984	100.0

Mean	2.172	Std. err.	0.036
Mode	2.000	Std. dev.	1.123
Kurtosis	-0.983	Skewness	0.370
Median	2.006	Variance	1.261

Range for computation of statistics: 1 through 4.

Q. 3(g).   Too many laws to expect to obey all. [19]

TABLE II-3(g):   GROUP II (Fall, 1972).

Category Label	n	%
0. No response	12	1.3
1. Agree a lot	209	22.9
2. Agree a little	284	31.1
3. Disagree a little	238	26.0
4. Disagree a lot	171	18.7
TOTAL	914	100.0

Mean	2.380	Std. err.	0.035
Mode	2.000	Std. dev.	1.071
Kurtosis	-1.034	Skewness	0.052
Median	2.331	Variance	1.147

Range for computation of statistics: 1 through 4.

TABLE III-3(g):   GROUP III (Spring, 1973).

Category Label	n	%
0. No response	9	0.9
1. Agree a lot	191	19.4
2. Agree a little	294	29.9
3. Disagree a little	270	27.4
4. Disagree a lot	220	22.4
TOTAL	984	100.0

Mean	2.509	Std. err.	0.034
Mode	2.000	Std. dev.	1.068
Kurtosis	-1.071	Skewness	-0.064
Median	2.493	Variance	1.141

Range for computation of statistics: 1 through 4.

Q. 3(h). Better to obey bad law than try change.[20]

TABLE II-3(h): GROUP II (Fall, 1972).

Category Label	n	%
0. No response	12	1.3
1. Disagree a lot	202	22.1
2. Disagree a little	171	18.7
3. Agree a little	238	26.0
4. Agree a lot	291	31.8
TOTAL	914	100.0

Mean	2.650	Std. err.	0.039
Mode	4.000	Std. dev.	1.178
Kurtosis	-1.240	Skewness	-0.303
Median	2.803	Variance	1.387

Range for computation of statistics: 1 through 4.

TABLE III-3(h): GROUP III (Spring, 1973).

Category Label	n	%
0. No response	8	0.8
1. Disagree a lot	225	22.9
2. Disagree a little	188	19.1
3. Agree a little	258	26.2
4. Agree a lot	305	31.0
TOTAL	984	100.0

Mean	2.637	Std. err.	0.037
Mode	4.000	Std. dev.	1.166
Kurtosis	-1.296	Skewness	-0.256
Median	2.775	Variance	1.359

Range for computation of statistics: 1 through 4.

Q. 3(i). All suffer if don't respect the law.[21]

TABLE II-3(i): GROUP II (Fall, 1972).

Category Label	n	%
0. No response	9	1.0
1. Disagree a lot	119	13.0
2. Disagree a little	180	19.7
3. Agree a little	302	33.0
4. Agree a lot	304	33.3
TOTAL	914	100.0

Mean	2.846	Std. err.	0.035
Mode	4.000	Std. dev.	1.057
Kurtosis	-0.712	Skewness	-0.553
Median	2.993	Variance	1.116

Range for computation of statistics: 1 through 4.

TABLE III-3(i): GROUP III (Spring, 1973).

Category Label	n	%
0. No response	6	0.6
1. Disagree a lot	108	11.0
2. Disagree a little	185	18.8
3. Agree a little	359	36.5
4. Agree a lot	326	33.1
TOTAL	984	100.0

Mean	2.905	Std. err.	0.032
Mode	3.000	Std. dev.	1.003
Kurtosis	-0.540	Skewness	-0.610
Median	3.038	Variance	1.005

Range for computation of statistics: 1 through 4.

Q. 3(j).   Times when justified in bending law. [22]

TABLE II-3(j):   GROUP II (Fall, 1973).

Category Label	n	%
0. No response	11	1.2
1. Agree a lot	327	35.8
2. Agree a little	436	47.7
3. Disagree a little	92	10.1
4. Disagree a lot	48	5.3
TOTAL	914	100.0

Mean	1.824	Std. err.	0.027
Mode	2.000	Std. dev.	0.828
Kurtosis	0.546	Skewness	0.765
Median	1.773	Variance	0.686

Range for computation of statistics: 1 through 4.

TABLE III-3(j):   GROUP III (Spring, 1973).

Category Label	n	%
0. No response	10	1.0
1. Agree a lot	406	41.3
2. Agree a little	431	43.8
3. Disagree a little	88	8.9
4. Disagree a lot	49	5.0
TOTAL	984	100.0

Mean	1.756	Std. err.	0.026
Mode	2.000	Std. dev.	0.826
Kurtosis	0.668	Skewness	0.900
Median	1.676	Variance	0.683

Range for computation of statistics: 1 through 4.

Q. 3(k). OK to disobey law if against religion.[23]

TABLE II-3(k): GROUP II (Fall, 1972).

Category Label	n	%
0. No response	18	2.0
1. Agree a lot	240	26.3
2. Agree a little	259	28.3
3. Disagree a little	219	24.0
4. Disagree a lot	178	19.5
TOTAL	914	100.0

Mean	2.327	Std. err.	0.037
Mode	2.000	Std. dev.	1.120
Kurtosis	-1.110	Skewness	0.080
Median	2.268	Variance	1.254

Range for computation of statistics: 1 through 4.

TABLE III-3(k): GROUP III (Spring, 1973).

Category Label	n	%
0. No response	19	1.9
1. Agree a lot	207	21.0
2. Agree a little	282	28.7
3. Disagree a little	245	24.9
4. Disagree a lot	231	23.5
TOTAL	984	100.0

Mean	2.470	Std. err.	0.036
Mode	2.000	Std. dev.	1.121
Kurtosis	-1.084	Skewness	-0.078
Median	2.443	Variance	1.256

Range for computation of statistics: 1 through 4.

Q 3(1).   OK to disobey law in an emergency. [24]

TABLE II-3(1):   GROUP II (Fall, 1972).

Category Label	n	%
0. No response	10	1.1
1. Agree a lot	624	68.3
2. Agree a little	211	23.1
3. Disagree a little	47	5.1
4. Disagree a lot	22	2.4
TOTAL	914	100.0

Mean	1.395	Std. err.	0.024
Mode	1.000	Std. dev.	0.713
Kurtosis	2.953	Skewness	1.704
Median	1.216	Variance	0.509

Range for computation of statistics: 1 through 4.

TABLE III-3(1):   GROUP III (Spring, 1973).

Category Label	n	%
0. No response	10	1.0
1. Agree a lot	669	68.0
2. Agree a little	221	22.5
3. Disagree a little	57	5.8
4. Disagree a lot	27	2.7
TOTAL	984	100.0

Mean	1.413	Std. err.	0.024
Mode	1.000	Std. dev.	0.737
Kurtosis	2.704	Skewness	1.688
Median	1.220	Variance	0.544

Range for computation of statistics: 1 through 4.

Q. 3(m).   Can have no justice unless obey law. [25]

TABLE II-3(m):   GROUP II (Fall, 1972).

Category Label		n	%
0.	No response	17	1.9
1.	Disagree a lot	80	8.8
2.	Disagree a little	139	15.2
3.	Agree a little	216	23.6
4.	Agree a lot	462	50.5
TOTAL		914	100.0

Mean	3.123	Std. err.	0.036
Mode	4.000	Std. dev.	1.078
Kurtosis	0.033	Skewness	-1.022
Median	3.511	Variance	1.161

Range for computation of statistics: 1 through 4.

TABLE III-3(m):   GROUP III (Spring, 1973).

Category Label		n	%
0.	No response	25	2.5
1.	Disagree a lot	89	9.0
2.	Disagree a little	149	15.1
3.	Agree a little	288	29.3
4.	Agree a lot	433	44.0
TOTAL		914	100.0

Mean	3.032	Std. err.	0.035
Mode	4.000	Std. dev.	1.087
Kurtosis	0.041	Skewness	-0.960
Median	3.295	Variance	1.182

Range for computation of statistics: 1 through 4.

Q. 3(n). Wrong disobey law though against conscience.[26]

TABLE II-3(n): GROUP II (Fall, 1972).

Category Label	n	%
0. No response	9	1.0
1. Disagree a lot	105	11.5
2. Disagree a little	161	17.6
3. Agree a little	304	33.3
4. Agree a lot	335	36.7
TOTAL	914	100.0

Mean	2.931	Std. err.	0.034
Mode	4.000	Std. dev.	1.043
Kurtosis	−0.514	Skewness	−0.680
Median	3.099	Variance	1.087

Range for computation of statistics: 1 through 4.

TABLE III-3(n): GROUP III (Spring, 1973).

Category Label	n	%
0. No response	9	0.9
1. Disagree a lot	106	10.8
2. Disagree a little	195	19.8
3. Agree a little	331	33.6
4. Agree a lot	343	34.9
TOTAL	984	100.0

Mean	2.908	Std. err.	0.033
Mode	4.000	Std. dev.	1.026
Kurtosis	−0.550	Skewness	−0.617
Median	3.050	Variance	1.052

Range for computation of statistics: 1 through 4.

Q. 3(o). Most laws are for good of all.[27]

TABLE II-3(o): GROUP II (Fall, 1972).

Category Label	n	%
0. No response	12	1.3
1. Disagree a lot	95	10.4
2. Disagree a little	149	16.3
3. Agree a little	302	33.0
4. Agree a lot	356	38.9
TOTAL	914	100.0

Mean	2.979	Std. err.	0.034
Mode	4.000	Std. dev.	1.043
Kurtosis	-0.288	Skewness	-0.788
Median	3.166	Variance	1.087

Range for computation of statistics: 1 through 4.

TABLE III-3(o): GROUP III (Spring, 1973).

Category Label	n	%
0. No response	13	1.3
1. Disagree a lot	93	9.5
2. Disagree a little	175	17.8
3. Agree a little	350	35.6
4. Agree a lot	353	35.9
TOTAL	984	100.0

Mean	2.952	Std. err.	0.032
Mode	4.000	Std. dev.	1.016
Kurtosis	-0.224	Skewness	-0.748
Median	3.103	Variance	1.032

Range for computation of statistics: 1 through 4.

Obligation Index Score (Absolute), 4 levels.
(See Coding Outline, page 32).

TABLE II-3(f)-3(o): GROUP II (Fall, 1972).

Category Label	n	%
0. No response	72	7.9
1. Low	17	1.9
2. Slight	291	31.8
3. Moderate	517	56.6
4. High	17	1.9
TOTAL	914	100.0

Mean	2.634	Std. err.	0.019
Mode	3.000	Std. dev.	0.560
Kurtosis	-0.129	Skewness	-0.542
Median	2.719	Variance	0.313

Range for computation of statistics: 1 through 4.

TABLE III-3(f)-3(o): GROUP III (Spring, 1973).

Category Label	n	%
0. No response	73	7.4
1. Low	13	1.3
2. Slight	322	32.7
3. Moderate	553	56.2
4. High	23	2.3
TOTAL	984	100.0

Mean	2.643	Std. err.	0.018
Mode	3.000	Std. dev.	0.556
Kurtosis	-0.272	Skewness	-0.389
Median	2.718	Variance	0.309

Range for computation of statistics: 1 through 4.

Obligation Index Score (Absolute), 2 levels.
(See Coding Outline, page 32).

TABLE II-3(f)-3(o): GROUP II (Fall, 1972).

Category Label	n	%
0. No response	72	7.9
1. Not obligated	308	33.7
2. Obligated	534	58.4
TOTAL	914	100.0

Mean	1.634	Std. err.	0.017
Mode	2.000	Std. dev.	0.482
Kurtosis	-1.691	Skewness	-0.557
Median	1.712	Variance	0.232

Range for computation of statistics: 1 through 2.

TABLE III-3(f)-3(o): GROUP III (Spring, 1973).

Category Label	n	%
0. No response	73	7.4
1. Not obligated	335	34.0
2. Obligated	576	58.5
TOTAL	984	100.0

Mean	1.632	Std. err.	0.016
Mode	2.000	Std. dev.	0.482
Kurtosis	-1.700	Skewness	-0.548
Median	1.709	Variance	0.233

Range for computation of statistics: 1 through 2.

Obligation Index Score (Relative), 4 levels.
(See Coding Outline, page 25).

TABLE II-3(f)-3(o):   GROUP II (Fall, 1972).

Category Label	n	%
0. No response	72	7.9
1. Low	235	25.7
2. Slight	235	25.7
3. Moderate	263	28.8
4. High	109	11.9
TOTAL	914	100.0

Mean	2.292	Std. err.	0.035
Mode	3.000	Std. dev.	1.012
Kurtosis	-1.133	Skewness	0.141
Median	2.291	Variance	1.025

Range for computation of statistics: 1 through 4.

TABLE III-3(f)-3(o): GROUP III (Spring, 1973).

Category Label	n	%
0. No response	73	7.4
1. Low	276	28.0
2. Slight	216	22.0
3. Moderate	295	30.0
4. High	124	12.6
TOTAL	984	100.0

Mean	2.293	Std. err.	0.035
Mode	3.000	Std. dev.	1.042
Kurtosis	-1.232	Skewness	0.115
Median	2.331	Variance	1.087

Range for computation of statistics: 1 through 4.

Obligation Index Score (Relative), 2 levels.
(See Coding Outline, page 25).

TABLE II-3(f)-3(o): GROUP II (Fall, 1972).

Category Label	n	%
0. No response	72	7.9
1. Not obligated	470	51.4
2. Obligated	372	40.7
TOTAL	914	100.0

Mean	1.442	Std. err.	0.017
Mode	1.000	Std. dev.	0.497
Kurtosis	-1.946	Skewness	0.234
Median	1.396	Variance	0.247

Range for computation of statistics: 1 through 2.

TABLE III-3(f)-3(o): GROUP III (Spring, 1973).

Category Label	n	%
0. No response	73	7.4
1. Not obligated	492	50.0
2. Obligated	419	42.6
TOTAL	984	100.0

Mean	1.460	Std. err.	0.017
Mode	1.000	Std. dev.	0.499
Kurtosis	-1.975	Skewness	0.161
Median	1.426	Variance	0.249

Range for computation of statistics: 1 through 2.

PERSONALITY VARIABLES

Q. 3(p).   If try to change usually make worse.[28]

TABLE II-3(p):   GROUP II (Fall, 1972).

Category Label	n	%
0. No response	17	1.9
1. Disagree a lot	267	29.2
2. Disagree a little	261	28.6
3. Agree a little	247	27.0
4. Agree a lot	122	13.3
TOTAL	914	100.0

Mean	2.208	Std. err.	0.035
Mode	1.000	Std. dev.	1.062
Kurtosis	−0.998	Skewness	0.154
Median	2.163	Variance	1.129

Range for computation of statistics: 1 through 4.

TABLE III-3(p):   GROUP III (Spring, 1973).

Category Label	n	%
0. No response	14	1.4
1. Disagree a lot	301	30.6
2. Disagree a little	320	32.5
3. Agree a little	242	24.6
4. Agree a lot	107	10.9
TOTAL	984	100.0

Mean	2.129	Std. err.	0.032
Mode	2.000	Std. dev.	1.014
Kurtosis	−0.856	Skewness	0.285
Median	2.053	Variance	1.028

Range for computation of statistics: 1 through 4.

Q. 3(q). If grows up over time has much wisdom.[29]

TABLE II-3(q): GROUP II (Fall, 1972).

Category Label	n	%
0. No response	22	2.4
1. Disagree a lot	172	18.8
2. Disagree a little	257	28.1
3. Agree a little	329	36.0
4. Agree a lot	134	14.7
TOTAL	914	100.0

Mean	2.417	Std. err.	0.034
Mode	3.000	Std. dev.	1.029
Kurtosis	-0.720	Skewness	-0.223
Median	2.518	Variance	1.058

Range for computation of statistics: 1 through 4.

TABLE III-3(q): GROUP III (Spring, 1972).

Category Label	n	%
0. No response	26	2.6
1. Disagree a lot	213	21.6
2. Disagree a little	311	31.6
3. Agree a little	314	31.9
4. Agree a lot	120	12.2
TOTAL	984	100.0

Mean	2.294	Std. err.	0.033
Mode	3.000	Std. dev.	1.022
Kurtosis	-0.746	Skewness	-0.073
Median	2.314	Variance	1.044

Range for computation of statistics: 1 through 4.

Q. 3(r).   Should stick by what you have. [30]

TABLE II-3(r):   GROUP II (Fall, 1972).

Category Label		n	%
0.	No response	14	1.5
1.	Disagree a lot	301	32.9
2.	Disagree a little	260	28.4
3.	Agree a little	201	22.0
4.	Agree a lot	138	15.1
TOTAL		914	100.0
Mean	2.162	Std. err.	0.036
Mode	1.000	Std. dev.	1.091
Kurtosis	−1.042	Skewness	0.304
Median	2.046	Variance	1.190

Range for computation of statistics: 1 through 4.

TABLE III-3(r):   GROUP III (Spring, 1973).

Category Label		n	%
0.	No response	11	1.1
1.	Disagree a lot	361	36.7
2.	Disagree a little	296	30.1
3.	Agree a little	193	19.6
4.	Agree a lot	123	12.5
TOTAL		984	100.0
Mean	2.057	Std. err.	0.034
Mode	1.000	Std. dev.	1.051
Kurtosis	−0.875	Skewness	0.475
Median	1.905	Variance	1.106

Range for computation of statistics: 1 through 4.

Q. 3(s). Must respect work of forefathers.[31]

TABLE II-3(s): GROUP II (Fall, 1972).

Category Label	n	%
0. No response	12	1.3
1. Disagree a lot	381	41.7
2. Disagree a little	271	29.6
3. Agree a little	167	18.3
4. Agree a lot	83	9.1
TOTAL	914	100.0

Mean	1.921	Std. err.	0.033
Mode	1.000	Std. dev.	1.005
Kurtosis	-0.624	Skewness	0.617
Median	1.736	Variance	1.010

Range for computation of statistics: 1 through 4.

TABLE III-3(s): GROUP III (Spring, 1973).

Category Label	n	%
0. No response	6	0.6
1. Disagree a lot	463	47.1
2. Disagree a little	288	29.3
3. Agree a little	153	15.5
4. Agree a lot	74	7.5
TOTAL	984	100.0

Mean	1.823	Std. err.	0.031
Mode	1.000	Std. dev.	0.960
Kurtosis	-0.320	Skewness	0.828
Median	1.580	Variance	0.921

Range for computation of statistics: 1 through 4.

Q. 3(t). Have little wisdom until along in years. [32]

TABLE II-3(t): GROUP II (Fall, 1972).

Category Label	n	%
0. No response	12	1.3
1. Disagree a lot	354	38.7
2. Disagree a little	280	30.6
3. Agree a little	184	20.1
4. Agree a lot	84	9.2
TOTAL	914	100.0

Mean	1.972	Std. err.	0.033
Mode	1.000	Std. dev.	1.005
Kurtosis	-0.714	Skewness	0.524
Median	1.825	Variance	1.009

Range for computation of statistics: 1 through 4.

TABLE III-3(t): GROUP III (Spring, 1973).

Category Label	n	%
0. No response	5	0.5
1. Disagree a lot	445	45.2
2. Disagree a little	291	29.6
3. Agree a little	169	17.2
4. Agree a lot	74	7.5
TOTAL	984	100.0

Mean	1.860	Std. err.	0.031
Mode	1.000	Std. dev.	0.962
Kurtosis	-0.462	Skewness	0.755
Median	1.644	Variance	0.926

Range for computation of statistics: 1 through 4.

Conservatism Index Score (Absolute), 4 levels.
(See Coding Outline, page 33).

TABLE II-3(p)-3(t): GROUP II (Fall, 1972).

Category Label	n	%
0. No response	52	5.7
1. Low	169	18.5
2. Slight	405	44.3
3. Moderate	261	28.6
4. High	27	3.0
TOTAL	914	100.0

Mean	2.169	Std. err.	0.026
Mode	2.000	Std. dev.	0.772
Kurtosis	-0.569	Skewness	0.109
Median	2.147	Variance	0.596

Range for computation of statistics: 1 through 4.

TABLE III-3(p)-3(t): GROUP III (Spring, 1973).

Category Label	n	%
0. No response	41	4.2
1. Low	214	21.7
2. Slight	489	49.7
3. Moderate	217	22.1
4. High	23	2.3
TOTAL	984	100.0

Mean	2.052	Std. err.	0.024
Mode	2.000	Std. dev.	0.743
Kurtosis	-0.327	Skewness	0.273
Median	2.027	Variance	0.552

Range for computation of statistics: 1 through 4.

Conservatism Index Score (Absolute), 2 levels.
(See Coding Outline, page 33).

TABLE II-3(p)-3(t):   GROUP II (Fall, 1972).

Category Label	n	%
0. No response	52	5.7
1. Not conservative	574	62.8
2. Conservative	288	31.5
TOTAL	914	100.0

Mean	1.334	Std. err.	0.016
Mode	1.000	Std. dev.	0.472
Kurtosis	−1.507	Skewness	0.703
Median	1.251	Variance	0.223

Range for computation of statistics: 1 through 2.

TABLE III-3(p)-3(t):   GROUP III (Spring, 1973).

Category Label	n	%
0. No response	41	4.2
1. Not conservative	703	71.4
2. Conservative	240	24.4
TOTAL	984	100.0

Mean	1.255	Std. err.	0.014
Mode	1.000	Std. dev.	0.436
Kurtosis	−0.732	Skewness	1.127
Median	1.171	Variance	0.190

Range for computation of statistics: 1 through 2.

Conservatism Index Score (Relative), 4 levels.
(See Coding Outline, page 26).

TABLE II-3(p)-3(t): GROUP II (Fall, 1972).

Category Label	n	%
0. No response	52	5.7
1. Low	169	18.5
2. Slight	146	16.0
3. Moderate	182	19.9
4. High	365	39.9
TOTAL	914	100.0

Mean	2.862	Std. err.	0.040
Mode	4.000	Std. dev.	1.166
Kurtosis	-1.288	Skewness	-0.473
Median	3.137	Variance	1.360

Range for computation of statistics: 1 through 4.

TABLE II-3(p)-3(t): GROUP III (Spring, 1973).

Category Label	n	%
0. No response	41	4.2
1. Low	214	21.7
2. Slight	186	18.9
3. Moderate	217	22.1
4. High	326	33.1
TOTAL	984	100.0

Mean	2.695	Std. err.	0.038
Mode	4.000	Std. dev.	1.166
Kurtosis	-1.415	Skewness	-0.250
Median	2.829	Variance	1.359

Range for computation of statistics: 1 through 4.

Conservatism Index Score (Relative), 2 levels.
(See Coding Outline, page 26).

TABLE II-3(p)-3(t): GROUP II (Fall, 1972).

Category Label	n	%
0. No response	52	5.7
1. Not conservative	315	34.5
2. Conservative	547	59.8
TOTAL	914	100.0

Mean	1.635	Std. err.	0.016
Mode	2.000	Std. dev.	0.482
Kurtosis	-1.689	Skewness	-0.559
Median	1.712	Variance	0.232

Range for computation of statistics: 1 through 2.

TABLE III-3(p)-3(t): GROUP III (Spring, 1973).

Category Label	n	%
0. No response	41	4.2
1. Not conservative	400	40.7
2. Conservative	543	55.2
TOTAL	984	100.0

Mean	1.576	Std. err.	0.016
Mode	2.000	Std. dev.	0.494
Kurtosis	-1.907	Skewness	-0.307
Median	1.632	Variance	0.245

Range for computation of statistics: 1 through 2.

Q. 3(u). Don't know who can count on.[33]

TABLE II-3(u): GROUP II (Fall, 1972).

Category Label	n	%
0. No response	28	3.1
1. Disagree a lot	36	3.9
2. Disagree a little	66	7.2
3. Agree a little	269	29.4
4. Agree a lot	515	56.3
TOTAL	914	100.0

Mean	3.321	Std. err.	0.033
Mode	4.000	Std. dev.	0.983
Kurtosis	2.575	Skewness	-1.698
Median	3.613	Variance	0.967

Range for computation of statistics: 1 through 4.

TABLE III-3(u): GROUP III (Spring, 1973).

Category Label	n	%
0. No response	25	2.5
1. Disagree a lot	40	4.1
2. Disagree a little	86	8.7
3. Agree a little	291	29.6
4. Agree a lot	542	55.1
TOTAL	984	100.0

Mean	3.306	Std. err.	0.031
Mode	4.000	Std. dev.	0.968
Kurtosis	2.210	Skewness	-1.584
Median	3.592	Variance	0.937

Range for computation of statistics: 1 through 4.

Q. 3(v). Average man's condition getting worse.[34]

TABLE II-3(v): GROUP II (Fall, 1972).

Category Label	n	%
0. No response	14	1.5
1. Disagree a lot	77	8.4
2. Disagree a little	187	20.5
3. Agree a little	339	37.1
4. Agree a lot	297	32.5
TOTAL	914	100.0

Mean	2.906	Std. err.	0.033
Mode	3.000	Std. dev.	0.998
Kurtosis	-0.171	Skewness	-0.690
Median	3.028	Variance	0.997

Range for computation of statistics: 1 through 4.

TABLE III-3(v): GROUP III (Spring, 1973).

Category Label	n	%
0. No response	11	1.1
1. Disagree a lot	72	7.3
2. Disagree a little	177	18.0
3. Agree a little	307	31.2
4. Agree a lot	417	42.4
TOTAL	984	100.0

Mean	3.064	Std. err.	0.032
Mode	4.000	Std. dev.	0.997
Kurtosis	-0.092	Skewness	-0.843
Median	3.256	Variance	0.994

Range for computation of statistics: 1 through 4.

Q. 3(w). Ought not to bring children into world.[35]

TABLE II-3(w): GROUP II (Fall, 1972).

Category Label	n	%
0. No response	16	1.8
1. Disagree a lot	300	32.8
2. Disagree a little	209	22.9
3. Agree a little	223	24.4
4. Agree a lot	166	18.2
TOTAL	914	100.0

Mean	2.244	Std. err.	0.038
Mode	1.000	Std. dev.	1.145
Kurtosis	-1.230	Skewness	0.171
Median	2.175	Variance	1.311

Range for computation of statistics: 1 through 4.

TABLE III-3(w): GROUP III (Spring, 1973),

Category Label	n	%
0. No response	12	1.2
1. Disagree a lot	319	32.4
2. Disagree a little	232	23.6
3. Agree a little	258	26.2
4. Agree a lot	163	16.6
TOTAL	984	100.0

Mean	2.245	Std. err.	0.035
Mode	1.000	Std. dev.	1.113
Kurtosis	-1.209	Skewness	0.175
Median	2.194	Variance	1.239

Range for computation of statistics: 1 through 4.

Q. 3(x).   Person has to live for today.[36]

TABLE II-3(x):   GROUP II (Fall, 1972).

Category Label	n	%
0. No response	15	1.6
1. Disagree a lot	149	16.3
2. Disagree a little	156	17.1
3. Agree a little	288	31.5
4. Agree a lot	306	33.5
TOTAL	914	100.0

Mean	2.789	Std. err.	0.037
Mode	4.000	Std. dev.	1.123
Kurtosis	-0.832	Skewness	-0.547
Median	2.976	Variance	1.262

Range for computation of statistics: 1 through 4.

TABLE III-3(x):   GROUP III (Spring, 1973).

Category Label	n	%
0. No response	13	1.3
1. Disagree a lot	172	17.5
2. Disagree a little	211	21.4
3. Agree a little	284	28.9
4. Agree a lot	304	30.9
TOTAL	984	100.0

Mean	2.705	Std. err.	0.036
Mode	4.000	Std. dev.	1.121
Kurtosis	-1.027	Skewness	-0.374
Median	2.838	Variance	1.256

Range for computation of statistics: 1 through 4.

Q. 3(y).   Not much use to vote.[37]

TABLE II-3(y): GROUP II (Fall, 1972).

Category Label	n	%
0. No response	15	1.6
1. Disagree a lot	384	42.0
2. Disagree a little	248	27.1
3. Agree a little	152	16.6
4. Agree a lot	115	12.6
TOTAL	914	100.0

Mean	1.965	Std. err.	0.036
Mode	1.000	Std. dev.	1.075
Kurtosis	−0.782	Skewness	0.599
Median	1.734	Variance	1.155

Range for computation of statistics: 1 through 4.

TABLE III-3(y): GROUP III (Spring, 1973).

Category Label	n	%
0. No response	15	1.5
1. Disagree a lot	367	37.3
2. Disagree a little	317	32.2
3. Agree a little	192	19.5
4. Agree a lot	93	9.5
TOTAL	984	100.0

Mean	1.981	Std. err.	0.032
Mode	1.000	Std. dev.	1.004
Kurtosis	−0.672	Skewness	0.509
Median	1.847	Variance	1.008

Range for computation of statistics: 1 through 4.

Alienation Index Score (Absolute), 4 levels.
(See Coding Outline, page 34).

TABLE II-3(u)-3(y): GROUP II (Fall, 1972).

Category Label	n	%
0. No response	51	5.6
1. Low	20	2.2
2. Slight	302	33.0
3. Moderate	466	51.0
4. High	75	8.2
TOTAL	914	100.0

Mean	2.691	Std. err.	0.022
Mode	3.000	Std. dev.	0.659
Kurtosis	-0.191	Skewness	-0.057
Median	2.735	Variance	0.434

Range for computation of statistics: 1 through 4.

TABLE III-3(u)-3(y): GROUP III (Spring, 1973).

Category Label	n	%
0. No response	57	5.8
1. Low	26	2.6
2. Slight	303	30.8
3. Moderate	504	51.2
4. High	94	9.6
TOTAL	984	100.0

Mean	2.718	Std. err.	0.022
Mode	3.000	Std. dev.	0.679
Kurtosis	-0.142	Skewness	-0.121
Median	2.767	Variance	0.462

Range for computation of statistics: 1 through 4.

Alienation Index Score (Absolute), 2 levels.
(See Coding Outline, page 34).

TABLE II-3(u)-3(y):   GROUP II (Fall, 1972).

Category Label	n	%
0. No response	51	5.6
1. Not alienated	322	35.2
2. Alienated	541	59.2
TOTAL	914	100.0

Mean	1.627	Std. err.	0.016
Mode	2.000	Std. dev.	0.484
Kurtosis	-1.726	Skewness	-0.524
Median	1.702	Variance	0.234

Range for computation of statistics: 1 through 2.

TABLE III-3(u)-3(y):   GROUP III (Spring, 1973).

Category Label	n	%
0. No response	57	5.8
1. Not alienated	329	33.4
2. Alienated	598	60.8
TOTAL	984	100.0

Mean	1.645	Std. err.	0.016
Mode	2.000	Std. dev.	0.479
Kurtosis	-1.634	Skewness	-0.606
Median	1.725	Variance	0.229

Range for computation of statistics: 1 through 2.

Alienation Index Score (Relative), 4 levels.
(See Coding Outline, page 27).

TABLE II-3(u)-3(y): GROUP II (Fall, 1972).

Category Label	n	%
0. No response	51	5.6
1. Low	81	8.9
2. Slight	152	16.6
3. Moderate	189	20.7
4. High	441	48.2
TOTAL	914	100.0

Mean	3.147	Std. err.	0.035
Mode	4.000	Std. dev.	1.021
Kurtosis	-0.630	Skewness	-0.827
Median	3.522	Variance	1.042

Range for computation of statistics: 1 through 4.

TABLE III-3(u)-3(y): GROUP III (Spring, 1973).

Category Label	n	%
0. No response	57	5.8
1. Low	93	9.5
2. Slight	137	13.9
3. Moderate	202	20.5
4. High	495	50.3
TOTAL	984	100.0

Mean	3.186	Std. err.	0.034
Mode	4.000	Std. dev.	1.025
Kurtosis	-0.442	Skewness	-0.937
Median	3.564	Variance	1.050

Range for computation of statistics: 1 through 4.

Alienation Index Score (Relative), 2 levels.
(See Coding Outline, page 27).

TABLE II-3(u)-3(y): GROUP II (Fall, 1972).

Category Label	n	%
0. No response	51	5.6
1. Not alienated	233	25.5
2. Alienated	630	68.9
TOTAL	914	100.0

Mean	1.730	Std. err.	0.015
Mode	2.000	Std. dev.	0.444
Kurtosis	-0.929	Skewness	-1.036
Median	1.815	Variance	0.197

Range for computation of statistics: 1 through 2.

TABLE III-3(u)-3(y): GROUP III (Spring, 1973).

Category Label	n	%
0. No response	57	5.8
1. Not alienated	230	23.4
2. Alienated	697	70.8
TOTAL	984	100.0

Mean	1.752	Std. err.	0.014
Mode	2.000	Std. dev.	0.432
Kurtosis	-0.642	Skewness	-1.166
Median	1.835	Variance	0.187

Range for computation of statistics: 1 through 2.

Q. 3(z). Artist and professor are more important.[38]

TABLE II-3(z): GROUP II (Fall, 1972).

Category Label	n	%
0. No response	21	2.3
1. Agree a lot	68	7.4
2. Agree a little	162	17.7
3. Disagree a little	304	33.3
4. Disagree a lot	359	39.3
TOTAL	914	100.0

Mean	2.998	Std. err.	0.034
Mode	4.000	Std. dev.	1.037
Kurtosis	0.126	Skewness	-0.891
Median	3.178	Variance	1.076

Range for computation of statistics: 1 through 4.

TABLE III-3(z): GROUP III (Spring, 1973).

Category Label	n	%
0. No response	18	1.8
1. Agree a lot	74	7.5
2. Agree a little	176	17.9
3. Disagree a little	319	32.4
4. Disagree a lot	397	40.3
TOTAL	984	100.0

Mean	3.019	Std. err.	0.033
Mode	4.000	Std. dev.	1.024
Kurtosis	0.039	Skewness	-0.869
Median	3.202	Variance	1.048

Range for computation of statistics: 1 through 4.

Q. 3(aa). There will always be war and conflict.[39]

TABLE II-3(aa): GROUP II (Fall, 1972).

Category Label	n	%
0. No response	18	2.0
1. Disagree a lot	195	21.3
2. Disagree a little	192	21.0
3. Agree a little	275	30.1
4. Agree a lot	234	25.6
TOTAL	914	100.0

Mean	2.560	Std. err.	0.038
Mode	3.000	Std. dev.	1.142
Kurtosis	-1.093	Skewness	-0.261
Median	2.689	Variance	1.305

Range for computation of statistics: 1 through 4.

TABLE III-3(aa): GROUP III (Spring, 1973).

Category Label	n	%
0. No response	7	0.7
1. Disagree a lot	218	22.2
2. Disagree a little	190	19.3
3. Agree a little	302	30.7
4. Agree a lot	267	27.1
TOTAL	984	100.0

Mean	2.614	Std. err.	0.036
Mode	3.000	Std. dev.	1.126
Kurtosis	-1.209	Skewness	-0.254
Median	2.755	Variance	1.267

Range for computation of statistics: 1 through 4.

Q. 3(bb). What young people need is discipline.[40]

TABLE II-3(bb): GROUP II (Fall, 1972).

Category Label	n	%
0. No response	17	1.9
1. Disagree a lot	331	36.2
2. Disagree a little	242	26.5
3. Agree a little	210	23.0
4. Agree a lot	114	12.5
TOTAL	914	100.0

Mean	2.080	Std. err.	0.036
Mode	1.000	Std. dev.	1.077
Kurtosis	-0.991	Skewness	0.351
Median	1.950	Variance	1.160

Range for computation of statistics: 1 through 4.

TABLE III-3(bb): GROUP III (Spring, 1973).

Category Label	n	%
0. No response	12	1.2
1. Disagree a lot	359	36.5
2. Disagree a little	238	24.2
3. Agree a little	232	23.6
4. Agree a lot	143	14.5
TOTAL	984	100.0

Mean	2.137	Std. err.	0.035
Mode	1.000	Std. dev.	1.101
Kurtosis	-1.133	Skewness	0.326
Median	2.008	Variance	1.213

Range for computation of statistics: 1 through 4.

Q. 3(cc). If don't get ahead not enough will power.[41]

TABLE II-3(cc): GROUP II (Fall, 1972),

Category Label	n	%
0. No response	19	2.1
1. Disagree a lot	286	31.3
2. Disagree a little	218	23.9
3. Agree a little	213	23.3
4. Agree a lot	178	19.5
TOTAL	914	100.0

Mean	2.268	Std. err.	0.038
Mode	1.000	Std. dev.	1.157
Kurtosis	-1.221	Skewness	0.141
Median	2.197	Variance	1.338

Range for computation of statistics: 1 through 4.

TABLE III-3(cc): GROUP III (Spring, 1973).

Category Label	n	%
0. No response	9	0.9
1. Disagree a lot	355	36.1
2. Disagree a little	269	27.3
3. Agree a little	204	20.7
4. Agree a lot	147	14.9
TOTAL	984	100.0

Mean	2.127	Std. err.	0.035
Mode	1.000	Std. dev.	1.090
Kurtosis	-1.063	Skewness	0.398
Median	1.976	Variance	1.187

Range for computation of statistics: 1 through 4.

Authoritarianism Index Score (Absolute), 4 levels.
(See Coding Outline, page 35).

TABLE II-3(aa)-3(cc): GROUP II (Fall, 1972).

Category Label	n	%
0. No response	29	3.2
1. Low	108	11.8
2. Slight	422	46.2
3. Moderate	291	31.8
4. High	64	7.0
TOTAL	914	100.0

Mean	2.351	Std. err.	0.026
Mode	2.000	Std. dev.	0.786
Kurtosis	-0.355	Skewness	0.190
Median	2.293	Variance	0.617

Range for computation of statistics: 1 through 4.

TABLE III-3(aa)-3(cc): GROUP III (Spring, 1973).

Category Label	n	%
0. No response	21	2.1
1. Low	137	13.9
2. Slight	444	45.1
3. Moderate	323	32.8
4. High	59	6.0
TOTAL	984	100.0

Mean	2.316	Std. err.	0.025
Mode	2.000	Std. dev.	0.790
Kurtosis	-0.433	Skewness	0.125
Median	2.276	Variance	0.624

Range for computation of statistics: 1 through 4.

Authoritarianism Index Score (Absolute), 2 levels.
(See Coding Outline, page 35).

TABLE II-3(aa)-3(cc):   GROUP II (Fall, 1972).

Category Label	n	%
0. No response	29	3.2
1. Not authoritarian	530	58.0
2. Authoritarian	355	38.8
TOTAL	914	100.0

Mean	1.401	Std. err.	0.016
Mode	1.000	Std. dev.	0.490
Kurtosis	-1.839	Skewness	0.403
Median	1.335	Variance	0.240

Range for computation of statistics: 1 through 2.

TABLE III-3(aa)-3(cc):   GROUP III (Spring, 1973).

Category Label	n	%
0. No response	21	2.1
1. Not authoritarian	581	59.0
2. Authoritarian	382	38.8
TOTAL	984	100.0

Mean	1.397	Std. err.	0.016
Mode	1.000	Std. dev.	0.489
Kurtosis	-1.823	Skewness	0.422
Median	1.329	Variance	0.240

Range for computation of statistics: 1 through 2.

Authoritarianism Index Score (Relative), 4 levels.
(See Coding Outline, page 28).

TABLE II-3(aa)-3(cc): GROUP II (Fall, 1972).

Category Label	n	%
0. No response	29	3.2
1. Low	203	22.2
2. Slight	327	35.8
3. Moderate	231	25.3
4. High	124	13.6
TOTAL	914	100.0

Mean	2.312	Std. err.	0.033
Mode	2.000	Std. dev.	0.977
Kurtosis	-0.936	Skewness	0.247
Median	2.232	Variance	0.955

Range for computation of statistics: 1 through 4.

TABLE III-3(aa)-3(cc): GROUP III (Spring, 1973).

Category Label	n	%
0. No response	21	2.1
1. Low	249	25.3
2. Slight	332	33.7
3. Moderate	251	25.5
4. High	131	13.3
TOTAL	984	100.0

Mean	2.274	Std. err.	0.032
Mode	2.000	Std. dev.	0.995
Kurtosis	-0.992	Skewness	0.262
Median	2.200	Variance	0.989

Range for computation of statistics: 1 through 4.

Authoritarianism Index Score (Relative), 2 levels.
(See Coding Outline, page 28).

TABLE II-3(aa)-3(cc): GROUP II (Fall, 1972).

Category Label	n	%
0. No response	29	3.2
1. Not authoritarian	530	58.0
2. Authoritarian	355	38.8
TOTAL	914	100.0

Mean	1.401	Std. err.	0.016
Mode	1.000	Std. dev.	0.490
Kurtosis	-1.839	Skewness	0.403
Median	1.335	Variance	0.240

Range for computation of statistics: 1 through 2.

TABLE III-3(aa)-3(cc): GROUP III (Spring, 1973).

Category Label	n	%
0. No response	21	2.1
1. Not authoritarian	581	59.0
2. Authoritarian	382	38.8
TOTAL	984	100.0

Mean	1.397	Std. err.	0.016
Mode	1.000	Std. dev.	0.489
Kurtosis	-1.823	Skewness	0.422
Median	1.329	Variance	0.240

Range for computation of statistics: 1 through 2.

Q. 7(a).   I would rather not plan ahead.[46]

TABLE II-7(a):   GROUP II (Fall, 1972).

Category Label	n	%
0. No response	14	1.5
1. Disagree a lot	271	29.6
2. Disagree a little	287	31.4
3. Agree a little	223	24.4
4. Agree a lot	119	13.0
TOTAL	914	100.0

Mean	2.177	Std. err.	0.035
Mode	2.000	Std. dev.	1.045
Kurtosis	-0.933	Skewness	0.246
Median	2.099	Variance	1.092

Range for computation of statistics: 1 through 4.

TABLE III-7(a):   GROUP III (Spring, 1973).

Category Label	n	%
0. No response	6	0.6
1. Disagree a lot	330	33.5
2. Disagree a little	327	33.2
3. Agree a little	230	23.4
4. Agree a lot	91	9.2
TOTAL	984	100.0

Mean	2.071	Std. err.	0.031
Mode	1.000	Std. dev.	0.979
Kurtosis	-0.816	Skewness	0.410
Median	1.977	Variance	0.959

Range for computation of statistics: 1 through 4.

Q. 7(b).   I have more bad luck than good.[47]

TABLE II-7(b):   GROUP II (Fall, 1972).

Category Label	n	%
0. No response	14	1.5
1. Disagree a lot	159	17.4
2. Disagree a little	283	31.0
3. Agree a little	286	31.3
4. Agree a lot	172	18.8
TOTAL	914	100.0

Mean	2.485	Std. err.	0.034
Mode	3.000	Std. dev.	1.033
Kurtosis	−0.837	Skewness	−0.129
Median	2.503	Variance	1.067

Range for computation of statistics: 1 through 4.

TABLE III-7(b):   GROUP III (Spring, 1973).

Category Label	n	%
0. No response	12	1.2
1. Disagree a lot	209	21.2
2. Disagree a little	349	35.5
3. Agree a little	257	26.1
4. Agree a lot	157	16.0
TOTAL	984	100.0

Mean	2.343	Std. err.	0.033
Mode	2.000	Std. dev.	1.022
Kurtosis	−0.873	Skewness	0.106
Median	2.277	Variance	1.044

Range for computation of statistics: 1 through 4.

Q. 7(c). Not much use to plan ahead.[48]

TABLE II-7(c): GROUP II (Fall, 1972).

Category Label	n	%
0. No response	15	1.6
1. Disagree a lot	167	18.3
2. Disagree a little	302	33.0
3. Agree a little	291	31.8
4. Agree a lot	139	15.2
TOTAL	914	100.0

Mean	2.407	Std. err.	0.033
Mode	2.000	Std. dev.	1.005
Kurtosis	-0.750	Skewness	-0.078
Median	2.411	Variance	1.011

Range for computation of statistics: 1 through 4.

TABLE III-7(c): GROUP III (Spring, 1973).

Category Label	n	%
0. No response	10	1.0
1. Disagree a lot	222	22.6
2. Disagree a little	321	32.6
3. Agree a little	296	30.1
4. Agree a lot	135	13.7
TOTAL	984	100.0

Mean	2.329	Std. err.	0.032
Mode	2.000	Std. dev.	1.004
Kurtosis	-0.896	Skewness	0.060
Median	2.310	Variance	1.008

Range for computation of statistics: 1 through 4.

Q. 7(d). No use to try to get ahead.[49]

TABLE II-7(d): GROUP II (Fall, 1972).

Category Label	n	%
0. No response	15	1.6
1. Disagree a lot	471	51.5
2. Disagree a little	204	22.3
3. Agree a little	170	18.6
4. Agree a lot	54	5.9
TOTAL	914	100.0

Mean	1.756	Std. err.	0.032
Mode	1.000	Std. dev.	0.972
Kurtosis	-0.456	Skewness	0.782
Median	1.438	Variance	0.945

Range for computation of statistics: 1 through 4.

TABLE III-7(d): GROUP II (Spring, 1973).

Category Label	n	%
0. No response	8	0.8
1. Disagree a lot	532	54.1
2. Disagree a little	184	18.7
3. Agree a little	191	19.4
4. Agree a lot	69	7.0
TOTAL	984	100.0

Mean	1.777	Std. err.	0.032
Mode	1.000	Std. dev.	1.000
Kurtosis	-0.570	Skewness	0.829
Median	1.410	Variance	0.999

Range for computation of statistics: 1 through 4.

Cynicism Index Score (Absolute), 4 levels.
(See Coding Outline, page 36).

TABLE II-7(a)-7(d):   GROUP II (Fall, 1972).

Category Label	n	%
0. No response	19	2.1
1. Low	168	18.4
2. Slight	476	52.1
3. Moderate	200	21.9
4. High	51	5.6
TOTAL	914	100.0

Mean	2.150	Std. err.	0.026
Mode	2.000	Std. dev.	0.786
Kurtosis	-0.077	Skewness	0.436
Median	2.087	Variance	0.617

Range for computation of statistics: 1 through 4.

TABLE III-7(a)-7(d):   GROUP III (Spring, 1973).

Category Label	n	%
0. No response	16	1.6
1. Low	234	23.8
2. Slight	492	50.0
3. Moderate	196	19.9
4. High	46	4.7
TOTAL	984	100.0

Mean	2.056	Std. err.	0.026
Mode	2.000	Std. dev.	0.795
Kurtosis	-0.141	Skewness	0.469
Median	2.008	Variance	0.632

Range for computation of statistics: 1 through 4.

Cynicism Index Score (Absolute), 2 levels.
(See Coding Outline, page 36).

TABLE II-7(a)-7(d):   GROUP II (Fall, 1972).

Category Label		n	%
0. No response		19	2.1
1. Not cynical		644	70.5
2. Cynical		251	27.5
TOTAL		914	100.0

Mean	1.280	Std. err.	0.015
Mode	1.000	Std. dev.	0.449
Kurtosis	-1.047	Skewness	0.977
Median	1.195	Variance	0.202

Range for computation of statistics: 1 through 2.

TABLE III-7(a)-7(d):   GROUP III (Spring, 1973).

Category Label		n	%
0. No response		16	1.6
1. Not cynical		726	73.8
2. Cynical		242	24.6
TOTAL		984	100.0

Mean	1.250	Std. err.	0.014
Mode	1.000	Std. dev.	0.433
Kurtosis	-0.669	Skewness	1.154
Median	1.167	Variance	0.188

Range for computation of statistics: 1 through 2.

Cynicism Index Score (Relative), 4 levels.
(See Coding Outline, page 29).

TABLE II-7(a)-7(d): GROUP II (Fall, 1972).

Category Label	n	%
0. No response	19	2.1
1. Low	168	18.4
2. Slight	250	27.4
3. Moderate	226	24.7
4. High	251	27.5
TOTAL	914	100.0

Mean	2.626	Std. err.	0.036
Mode	4.000	Std. dev.	1.083
Kurtosis	-1.280	Skewness	-0.106
Median	2.631	Variance	1.172

Range for computation of statistics: 1 through 4.

TABLE III-7(a)-7(d): GROUP III (Spring, 1973).

Category Label	n	%
0. No response	16	1.6
1. Low	234	23.8
2. Slight	251	25.5
3. Moderate	241	24.5
4. High	242	24.6
TOTAL	984	100.0

Mean	2.507	Std. err.	0.036
Mode	2.000	Std. dev.	1.111
Kurtosis	-1.345	Skewness	-0.000
Median	2.496	Variance	1.235

Range for computation of statistics: 1 through 4.

Cynicism Index Score (Relative), 2 levels.
(See Coding Outline, page 29).

TABLE II-7(a)-7(d): GROUP II (Fall, 1972).

Category Label	n	%
0. No response	19	2.1
1. Not cynical	418	45.7
2. Cynical	477	52.2
TOTAL	914	100.0

Mean	1.533	Std. err.	0.017
Mode	2.000	Std. dev.	0.499
Kurtosis	-1.984	Skewness	-0.132
Median	1.562	Variance	0.249

Range for computation of statistics: 1 through 2.

TABLE III-7(a)-7(d): GROUP III (Spring, 1973).

Category Label	n	%
0. No response	16	1.6
1. Not cynical	485	49.3
2. Cynical	483	49.1
TOTAL	984	100.0

Mean	1.499	Std. err.	0.016
Mode	1.000	Std. dev.	0.500
Kurtosis	-2.001	Skewness	0.004
Median	1.498	Variance	0.250

Range for computation of statistics: 1 through 2.

FEELINGS TOWARD
POLITICAL INTEREST GROUPS

Q. 4(a). American Legion.[43]

TABLE II-4(a): GROUP II (Fall, 1972).

Category Label	n	%
1. Very unfavorable	48	5.3
2. Quite unfavorable	44	4.8
3. Fairly unfavorable	36	3.9
4. More unfav. than fav.	52	5.7
5. More fav. than unfav.	118	12.9
6. Fairly favorable	131	14.3
7. Quite favorable	98	10.7
8. Very favorable	44	4.8
9. No feelings/don't know	343	37.5
TOTAL	914	100.0

Mean	5.019	Std. err.	0.084
Mode	6.000	Std. dev.	1.999
Kurtosis	-0.592	Skewness	-0.577
Median	5.394	Variance	3.998

Range for computation of statistics: 1 through 8.

TABLE III-4(a): GROUP III (Spring, 1973).

Category Label	n	%
1. Very unfavorable	44	4.5
2. Quite unfavorable	32	3.3
3. Fairly unfavorable	34	3.5
4. More unfav. than fav.	42	4.3
5. More fav. than unfav.	127	12.9
6. Fairly favorable	113	11.5
7. Quite favorable	75	7.6
8. Very favorable	20	2.0
9. No feelings/don't know	497	50.5
TOTAL	984	100.0

Mean	4.879	Std. err.	0.086
Mode	5.000	Std. dev.	1.901
Kurtosis	-0.446	Skewness	-0.630
Median	5.220	Variance	3.613

Range for computation of statistics: 1 through 8.

Q. 4(b).   Labor Unions.[43]

TABLE II-4(b):   GROUP II (Fall, 1972).

Category Label	n	%
1. Very unfavorable	15	1.6
2. Quite unfavorable	12	1.3
3. Fairly unfavorable	14	1.5
4. More unfav. than fav.	40	4.4
5. More fav. than unfav.	146	16.0
6. Fairly favorable	185	20.2
7. Quite favorable	271	29.6
8. Very favorable	136	14.9
9. No feelings/don't know	95	10.4
TOTAL	914	100.0

Mean	6.186	Std. err.	0.052
Mode	7.000	Std. dev.	1.478
Kurtosis	1.813	Skewness	-1.185
Median	6.486	Variance	2.183

Range for computation of statistics: 1 through 8.

TABLE III-4(b):   GROUP III (Spring, 1973).

Category Label	n	%
1. Very unfavorable	15	1.5
2. Quite unfavorable	7	0.7
3. Fairly unfavorable	23	2.3
4. More unfav. than fav.	35	3.6
5. More fav. than unfav.	147	14.9
6. Fairly favorable	229	23.3
7. Quite favorable	277	28.2
8. Very favorable	148	15.0
9. No feelings/don't know	103	10.5
TOTAL	984	100.0

Mean	6.209	Std. err.	0.048
Mode	7.000	Std. dev.	1.435
Kurtosis	1.949	Skewness	-1.175
Median	6.432	Variance	2.059

Range for computation of statistics: 1 through 8.

FEELINGS TOWARD INTEREST GROUPS

Q. 4(c).   Black Panthers.[43]

TABLE II-4(c):   GROUP II   (Fall, 1972).

Category Label	n	%
1. Very unfavorable	27	3.0
2. Quite unfavorable	13	1.4
3. Fairly unfavorable	7	0.8
4. More unfav. than fav.	37	4.0
5. More fav. than unfav.	91	10.0
6. Fairly favorable	134	14.7
7. Quite favorable	261	28.6
8. Very favorable	283	31.0
9. No feelings/don't know	61	6.7
TOTAL	914	100.0

Mean	6.532	Std. err.	0.057
Mode	8.000	Std. dev.	1.656
Kurtosis	2.498	Skewness	-1.581
Median	6.950	Variance	2.742

Range for computation of statistics: 1 through 8.

TABLE III-4(c):   GROUP III (Spring, 1973).

Category Label	n	%
1. Very unfavorable	30	3.0
2. Quite unfavorable	17	1.7
3. Fairly unfavorable	19	1.9
4. More unfav. than fav.	52	5.3
5. More fav. than unfav.	125	12.7
6. Fairly favorable	182	18.5
7. Quite favorable	259	26.3
8. Very favorable	222	22.6
9. No feelings/don't know	78	7.9
TOTAL	984	100.0

Mean	6.220	Std. err.	0.057
Mode	7.000	Std. dev.	1.704
Kurtosis	1.394	Skewness	-1.249
Median	6.608	Variance	2.905

Range for computation of statistics: 1 through 8.

Q. 4(d). College professors.[43]

TABLE II-4(d): GROUP II (Fall, 1972).

Category Label	n	%
1. Very unfavorable	14	1.5
2. Quite unfavorable	16	1.8
3. Fairly unfavorable	18	2.0
4. More unfav. than fav.	41	4.5
5. More fav. than unfav.	151	16.5
6. Fairly favorable	230	25.2
7. Quite favorable	264	28.9
8. Very favorable	106	11.6
9. No feelings/don't know	74	8.1
TOTAL	914	100.0

Mean	6.065	Std. err.	0.050
Mode	7.000	Std. dev.	1.451
Kurtosis	1.782	Skewness	-1.160
Median	6.283	Variance	2.107

Range for computation of statistics: 1 through 8.

TABLE III-4(d): GROUP III (Spring, 1973).

Category Label	n	%
1. Very unfavorable	3	0.3
2. Quite unfavorable	9	0.9
3. Fairly unfavorable	21	2.1
4. More unfav. than fav.	44	4.5
5. More fav. than unfav.	156	15.9
6. Fairly favorable	275	27.9
7. Quite favorable	307	31.2
8. Very favorable	98	10.0
9. No feelings/don't know	71	7.2
TOTAL	984	100.0

Mean	6.159	Std. err.	0.041
Mode	7.000	Std. dev.	1.246
Kurtosis	1.287	Skewness	-0.914
Median	6.313	Variance	1.553

Range for computation of statistics: 1 through 8.

Q. 4(e). National Guard.[43]

TABLE II-4(e): GROUP II (Fall, 1972).

Category Label	n	%
1. Very unfavorable	85	9.3
2. Quite unfavorable	49	5.4
3. Fairly unfavorable	38	4.2
4. More unfav. than fav.	88	9.6
5. More fav. than unfav.	147	16.1
6. Fairly favorable	151	16.5
7. Quite favorable	150	16.4
8. Very favorable	81	8.9
9. No feelings/don't know	125	13.7
TOTAL	914	100.0

Mean	5.054	Std. err.	0.075
Mode	6.000	Std. dev.	2.113
Kurtosis	-0.684	Skewness	-0.564
Median	5.415	Variance	4.465

Range for computation of statistics: 1 through 8.

TABLE III-4(e): GROUP III (Spring, 1973).

Category Label	n	%
1. Very unfavorable	62	6.3
2. Quite unfavorable	40	4.1
3. Fairly unfavorable	31	3.2
4. More unfav. than fav.	102	10.4
5. More fav. than unfav.	159	16.2
6. Fairly favorable	183	18.6
7. Quite favorable	150	15.2
8. Very favorable	90	9.1
9. No feelings/don't know	167	17.0
TOTAL	984	100.0

Mean	5.271	Std. err.	0.068
Mode	6.000	Std. dev.	1.953
Kurtosis	-0.245	Skewness	-0.679
Median	5.579	Variance	3.813

Range for computation of statistics: 1 through 8.

Q. 4(f). Mexican-Americans.[43]

TABLE II-4(f): GROUP II (Fall, 1972).

Category Label	n	%
1. Very unfavorable	18	2.0
2. Quite unfavorable	10	1.1
3. Fairly unfavorable	18	2.0
4. More unfav. than fav.	30	3.3
5. More fav. than unfav.	128	14.0
6. Fairly favorable	160	17.5
7. Quite favorable	184	20.1
8. Very favorable	9	10.6
9. No feelings/don't know	269	29.4
TOTAL	914	100.0

Mean	6.009	Std. err.	0.062
Mode	7.000	Std. dev.	1.572
Kurtosis	1.502	Skewness	-1.130
Median	6.241	Variance	2.472

Range for computation of statistics: 1 through 8.

TABLE III-4(f): GROUP III (Spring, 1973).

Category Label	n	%
1. Very unfavorable	11	1.1
2. Quite unfavorable	9	0.9
3. Fairly unfavorable	15	1.5
4. More unfav. than fav.	24	2.4
5. More fav. than unfav.	135	13.7
6. Fairly favorable	205	20.8
7. Quite favorable	234	23.8
8. Very favorable	105	10.7
9. No feelings/don't know	246	25.0
TOTAL	984	100.0

Mean	6.169	Std. err.	0.051
Mode	7.000	Std. dev.	1.387
Kurtosis	2.192	Skewness	-1.186
Median	6.354	Variance	1.924

Range for computation of statistics: 1 through 8.

Q. 4(g). Conservatives.[43]

TABLE II-4(g): GROUP II (Fall, 1972).

Category Label	n	%
1. Very unfavorable	100	10.9
2. Quite unfavorable	86	9.4
3. Fairly unfavorable	69	7.5
4. More unfav. than fav.	134	14.7
5. More fav. than unfav.	152	16.6
6. Fairly favorable	106	11.6
7. Quite favorable	75	8.2
8. Very favorable	25	2.7
9. No feelings/don't know	167	18.3
TOTAL	914	100.0

Mean	4.198	Std. err.	0.073
Mode	5.000	Std. dev.	1.983
Kurtosis	-0.953	Skewness	-0.100
Median	4.384	Variance	3.934

Range for computation of statistics: 1 through 8.

TABLE III-4(g): GROUP III (Spring, 1973).

Category Label	n	%
1. Very unfavorable	108	11.0
2. Quite unfavorable	67	6.8
3. Fairly unfavorable	59	6.0
4. More unfav. than fav.	188	19.1
5. More fav. than unfav.	146	14.8
6. Fairly favorable	122	12.4
7. Quite favorable	92	9.3
8. Very favorable	33	3.4
9. No feelings/don't know	169	17.2
TOTAL	984	100.0

Mean	4.345	Std. err.	0.069
Mode	4.000	Std. dev.	1.980
Kurtosis	-0.832	Skewness	-0.178
Median	4.423	Variance	3.922

Range for computation of statistics: 1 through 8.

Q. 4(h). Democrats.[43]

TABLE II-4(h): GROUP II (Fall, 1972).

Category Label	n	%
1. Very unfavorable	13	1.4
2. Quite unfavorable	16	1.8
3. Fairly unfavorable	15	1.6
4. More unfav. than fav.	23	2.5
5. More fav. than unfav.	118	12.9
6. Fairly favorable	162	17.7
7. Quite favorable	282	30.9
8. Very favorable	212	23.2
9. No feelings/don't know	73	8.0
TOTAL	914	100.0

Mean	6.438	Std. err.	0.052
Mode	7.000	Std. dev.	1.502
Kurtosis	2.211	Skewness	-1.383
Median	6.761	Variance	2.256

Range for computation of statistics: 1 through 8.

TABLE III-4(h): GROUP III (Spring, 1973).

Category Label	n	%
1. Very unfavorable	25	2.5
2. Quite unfavorable	13	1.3
3. Fairly unfavorable	6	0.6
4. More unfav. than fav.	22	2.2
5. More fav. than unfav.	136	13.8
6. Fairly favorable	211	21.4
7. Quite favorable	319	32.4
8. Very favorable	178	18.1
9. No feelings/don't know	74	7.5
TOTAL	984	100.0

Mean	6.330	Std. err.	0.050
Mode	7.000	Std. dev.	1.499
Kurtosis	3.098	Skewness	-1.548
Median	6.632	Variance	2.248

Range for computation of statistics: 1 through 8.

Q. 4(i).   Republicans.[43]

TABLE II-4(i):   GROUP II (Fall, 1972).

Category Label	n	%
1. Very unfavorable	168	18.4
2. Quite unfavorable	90	9.8
3. Fairly unfavorable	89	9.7
4. More unfav. than fav.	158	17.3
5. More fav. than unfav.	139	15.2
6. Fairly favorable	76	8.3
7. Quite favorable	50	5.5
8. Very favorable	10	1.1
9. No feelings/don't know	134	14.7
TOTAL	914	100.0

Mean	3.626	Std. err.	0.069
Mode	1.000	Std. dev.	1.931
Kurtosis	-0.998	Skewness	0.124
Median	3.772	Variance	3.729

Range for computation of statistics: 1 through 8.

TABLE III-4(i):   GROUP III (Spring, 1973).

Category Label	n	%
1. Very unfavorable	193	19.6
2. Quite unfavorable	105	10.7
3. Fairly unfavorable	107	10.9
4. More unfav. than fav.	205	20.8
5. More fav. than unfav.	149	15.1
6. Fairly favorable	66	6.7
7. Quite favorable	25	2.5
8. Very favorable	10	1.0
9. No feelings/don't know	124	12.6
TOTAL	984	100.0

Mean	3.419	Std. err.	0.061
Mode	4.000	Std. dev.	1.796
Kurtosis	-0.826	Skewness	0.168
Median	3.622	Variance	3.226

Range for computation of statistics: 1 through 8.

Q. 4(j). Liberals.[43]

TABLE II-4(j): GROUP II (Fall, 1972).

Category Label	n	%
1. Very unfavorable	25	2.7
2. Quite unfavorable	16	1.8
3. Fairly unfavorable	25	2.7
4. More unfav. than fav.	42	4.6
5. More fav. than unfav.	131	14.3
6. Fairly favorable	158	17.3
7. Quite favorable	239	26.1
8. Very favorable	162	17.7
9. No feelings/don't know	116	12.7
TOTAL	914	100.0

Mean	6.105	Std. err.	0.060
Mode	7.000	Std. dev.	1.693
Kurtosis	1.145	Skewness	-1.159
Median	6.508	Variance	2.865

Range for computation of statistics: 1 through 8.

TABLE III-4(j): GROUP III (Spring, 1973).

Category Label	n	%
1. Very unfavorable	31	3.2
2. Quite unfavorable	30	3.0
3. Fairly unfavorable	9	0.9
4. More unfav. than fav.	40	4.1
5. More fav. than unfav.	150	15.2
6. Fairly favorable	176	17.9
7. Quite favorable	270	27.4
8. Very favorable	142	14.4
9. No feelings/don't know	136	13.8
TOTAL	984	100.0

Mean	6.026	Std. err.	0.059
Mode	7.000	Std. dev.	1.712
Kurtosis	1.347	Skewness	-1.245
Median	6.432	Variance	2.932

Range for computation of statistics: 1 through 8.

Q. 4(k).   John Birch Society. [43]

TABLE II-4(k): GROUP II (Fall, 1972).

Category Label	n	%
1. Very unfavorable	214	23.4
2. Quite unfavorable	42	4.6
3. Fairly unfavorable	31	3.4
4. More unfav. than fav.	49	5.4
5. More fav. than unfav.	55	6.0
6. Fairly favorable	25	2.7
7. Quite favorable	23	2.5
8. Very favorable	2	0.2
9. No feelings/don't know	473	51.8
TOTAL	914	100.0

Mean	2.696	Std. err.	0.095
Mode	1.000	Std. dev.	2.005
Kurtosis	-0.762	Skewness	0.777
Median	1.655	Variance	4.021

Range for computation of statistics: 1 through 8.

TABLE III-4(k): GROUP III (Spring, 1973).

Category Label	n	%
1. Very unfavorable	229	23.3
2. Quite unfavorable	57	5.8
3. Fairly unfavorable	37	3.8
4. More unfav. than fav.	28	2.8
5. More fav. than unfav.	33	3.4
6. Fairly favorable	34	3.5
7. Quite favorable	13	1.3
8. Very favorable	8	0.8
9. No feelings/don't know	545	55.4
TOTAL	984	100.0

Mean	2.483	Std. err.	0.095
Mode	1.000	Std. dev.	1.987
Kurtosis	0.018	Skewness	1.134
Median	1.459	Variance	3.949

Range for computation of statistics: 1 through 8.

Q. 4(1). Women's Liberation.[43]

TABLE II-4(1): GROUP II (Fall, 1972).

Category Label	n	%
1. Very unfavorable	100	10.9
2. Quite unfavorable	39	4.3
3. Fairly unfavorable	29	3.2
4. More unfav. than fav.	72	7.9
5. More fav. than unfav.	165	18.1
6. Fairly favorable	136	14.9
7. Quite favorable	159	17.4
8. Very favorable	118	12.9
9. No feelings/don't know	96	10.5
TOTAL	914	100.0

Mean	5.197	Std. err.	0.077
Mode	5.000	Std. dev.	2.196
Kurtosis	−0.636	Skewness	−0.635
Median	5.529	Variance	4.824

Range for computation of statistics: 1 through 8.

TABLE III-4(1): GROUP III (Spring, 1973).

Category Label	n	%
1. Very unfavorable	98	10.0
2. Quite unfavorable	45	4.6
3. Fairly unfavorable	42	4.3
4. More unfav. than fav.	89	9.0
5. More fav. than unfav.	170	17.3
6. Fairly favorable	158	16.1
7. Quite favorable	170	17.3
8. Very favorable	89	9.0
9. No feelings/don't know	123	12.5
TOTAL	984	100.0

Mean	5.075	Std. err.	0.072
Mode	5.000	Std. dev.	2.120
Kurtosis	−0.643	Skewness	−0.594
Median	5.421	Variance	4.493

Range for computation of statistics: 1 through 8.

Q. 4(m). Government workers. [43]

TABLE II-4(m): GROUP II (Fall, 1972).

Category Label	n	%
1. Very unfavorable	22	2.4
2. Quite unfavorable	18	2.0
3. Fairly unfavorable	13	1.4
4. More unfav. than fav.	36	3.9
5. More fav. than unfav.	169	18.5
6. Fairly favorable	232	25.4
7. Quite favorable	205	22.4
8. Very favorable	79	8.6
9. No feelings/don't know	140	15.3
TOTAL	914	100.0

Mean	5.872	Std. err.	0.054
Mode	6.000	Std. dev.	1.516
Kurtosis	1.855	Skewness	-1.185
Median	6.056	Variance	2.298

Range for computation of statistics: 1 through 8.

TABLE III-4(m): GROUP III (Spring, 1972).

Category Label	n	%
1. Very unfavorable	23	2.3
2. Quite unfavorable	16	1.6
3. Fairly unfavorable	14	1.4
4. More unfav. than fav.	46	4.7
5. More fav. than unfav.	180	18.3
6. Fairly favorable	260	26.4
7. Quite favorable	216	22.0
8. Very favorable	86	8.7
9. No feelings/don't know	143	14.5
TOTAL	984	100.0

Mean	5.875	Std. err.	0.051
Mode	6.000	Std. dev.	1.491
Kurtosis	1.895	Skewness	-1.156
Median	6.044	Variance	2.224

Range for computation of statistics: 1 through 8.

Q. 4(n). Blue-collar workers.[43]

TABLE II-4(n): GROUP II (Fall, 1972).

Category Label	n	%
1. Very unfavorable	21	2.3
2. Quite unfavorable	9	1.0
3. Fairly unfavorable	13	1.4
4. More unfav. than fav.	39	4.3
5. More fav. than unfav.	146	16.0
6. Fairly favorable	205	22.4
7. Quite favorable	198	21.7
8. Very favorable	75	8.2
9. No feelings/don't know	208	22.8
TOTAL	914	100.0

Mean	5.921	Std. err.	0.056
Mode	6.000	Std. dev.	1.498
Kurtosis	1.986	Skewness	-1.197
Median	6.110	Variance	2.243

Range for computation of statistics: 1 through 8.

TABLE III-4(n): GROUP III (Spring, 1973).

Category Label	n	%
1. Very unfavorable	18	1.8
2. Quite unfavorable	7	0.7
3. Fairly unfavorable	9	0.9
4. More unfav. than fav.	41	4.2
5. More fav. than unfav.	143	14.5
6. Fairly favorable	233	23.7
7. Quite favorable	239	24.3
8. Very favorable	88	8.9
9. No feelings/don't know	206	20.9
TOTAL	984	100.0

Mean	6.058	Std. err.	0.050
Mode	7.000	Std. dev.	1.407
Kurtosis	2.522	Skewness	-1.264
Median	6.234	Variance	1.980

Range for computation of statistics: 1 through 8.

Q. 4(o). Policemen.[43]

TABLE II-4(o): GROUP II (Fall, 1972).

Category Label	n	%
1. Very unfavorable	115	12.6
2. Quite unfavorable	77	8.4
3. Fairly unfavorable	35	3.8
4. More unfav. than fav.	99	10.8
5. More fav. than unfav.	155	17.0
6. Fairly favorable	160	17.5
7. Quite favorable	133	14.6
8. Very favorable	53	5.8
9. No feelings/don't know	87	9.5
TOTAL	914	100.0

Mean	4.667	Std. err.	0.075
Mode	6.000	Std. dev.	2.159
Kurtosis	-0.995	Skewness	-0.396
Median	5.065	Variance	4.660

Range for computation of statistics: 1 through 8.

TABLE III-4(o): GROUP III (Spring, 1973).

Category Label	n	%
1. Very unfavorable	113	11.5
2. Quite unfavorable	64	6.5
3. Fairly unfavorable	48	4.9
4. More unfav. than fav.	129	13.1
5. More fav. than unfav.	181	18.4
6. Fairly favorable	169	17.2
7. Quite favorable	127	12.9
8. Very favorable	70	7.1
9. No feelings/don't know	83	8.4
TOTAL	984	100.0

Mean	4.738	Std. err.	0.070
Mode	5.000	Std. dev.	2.095
Kurtosis	-0.819	Skewness	-0.396
Median	5.033	Variance	4.389

Range for computation of statistics: 1 through 8.

TABLE II-4(p):   GROUP II (Fall, 1972).

Category Label	n	%
1. Very unfavorable	6	0.7
2. Quite unfavorable	3	0.3
3. Fairly unfavorable	2	0.2
4. More unfav. than fav.	1	0.1
5. More fav. than unfav.	18	2.0
6. Fairly favorable	22	2.4
7. Quite favorable	71	7.8
8. Very favorable	776	84.9
9. No feelings/don't know	15	1.6
TOTAL	914	100.0

Mean	7.730	Std. err.	0.030
Mode	8.000	Std. dev.	0.897
Kurtosis	27.818	Skewness	-4.850
Median	7.921	Variance	0.805

Range for computation of statistics: 1 through 8.

TABLE III-4(p):   GROUP III   (Spring, 1973).

Category Label	n	%
1. Very unfavorable	14	1.4
2. Quite unfavorable	1	0.1
3. Fairly unfavorable	0	0.0
4. More unfav. than fav.	1	0.1
5. More fav. than unfav.	13	1.3
6. Fairly favorable	22	2.2
7. Quite favorable	118	12.0
8. Very favorable	791	80.4
9. No feelings/don't know	24	2.4
TOTAL	984	100.0

Mean	7.678	Std. err.	0.032
Mode	8.000	Std. dev.	1.001
Kurtosis	28.060	Skewness	-4.951
Median	7.893	Variance	1.003

Range for computation of statistics: 1 through 8.

Q. 4(q). School teachers.[43]

TABLE II-4(q): GROUP II (Fall, 1972).

Category Label	n	%
1. Very unfavorable	12	1.3
2. Quite unfavorable	14	1.5
3. Fairly unfavorable	7	0.8
4. More unfav. than fav.	22	2.4
5. More fav. than unfav.	109	11.9
6. Fairly favorable	208	22.8
7. Quite favorable	331	36.2
8. Very favorable	155	17.0
9. No feelings/don't know	56	6.1
TOTAL	914	100.0

Mean	6.409	Std. err.	0.047
Mode	7.000	Std. dev.	1.363
Kurtosis	3.334	Skewness	-1.527
Median	6.672	Variance	1.857

Range for computation of statistics: 1 through 8.

TABLE III-4(q): GROUP III (Spring, 1973).

Category Label	n	%
1. Very unfavorable	10	1.0
2. Quite unfavorable	2	0.2
3. Fairly unfavorable	5	0.5
4. More unfav. than fav.	24	2.4
5. More fav. than unfav.	120	12.2
6. Fairly favorable	218	22.2
7. Quite favorable	376	38.2
8. Very favorable	181	18.4
9. No feelings/don't know	48	4.9
TOTAL	984	100.0

Mean	6.531	Std. err.	0.040
Mode	7.000	Std. dev.	1.214
Kurtosis	3.637	Skewness	-1.396
Median	6.737	Variance	1.475

Range for computation of statistics: 1 through 8.

Q. 4(r). Ku Klux Klan.[43]

TABLE II-4(r): GROUP II (Fall, 1972).

Category Label	n	%
1. Very unfavorable	792	86.7
2. Quite unfavorable	22	2.4
3. Fairly unfavorable	11	1.2
4. More unfav. than fav.	18	2.0
5. More fav. than unfav.	11	1.2
6. Fairly favorable	6	0.7
7. Quite favorable	4	0.4
8. Very favorable	4	0.4
9. No feelings/don't know	46	5.0
TOTAL	914	100.0

Mean	1.258	Std. err.	0.033
Mode	1.000	Std. dev.	0.982
Kurtosis	20.474	Skewness	4.413
Median	1.048	Variance	0.964

Range for computation of statistics: 1 through 8.

TABLE III-4(r): GROUP III (Spring, 1973).

Category Label	n	%
1. Very unfavorable	814	82.7
2. Quite unfavorable	37	3.8
3. Fairly unfavorable	14	1.4
4. More unfav. than fav.	17	1.7
5. More fav. than unfav.	9	0.9
6. Fairly favorable	6	0.6
7. Quite favorable	6	0.6
8. Very favorable	7	0.7
9. No feelings/don't know	74	7.5
TOTAL	984	100.0

Mean	1.293	Std. err.	0.035
Mode	1.000	Std. dev.	1.060
Kurtosis	19.873	Skewness	4.355
Median	1.059	Variance	1.123

Range for computation of statistics: 1 through 8.

Q. 4(s). Whites. [43]

TABLE II-4(s): GROUP II (Fall, 1972).

Category Label	n	%
1. Very unfavorable	210	23.0
2. Quite unfavorable	101	11.1
3. Fairly unfavorable	56	6.1
4. More unfav. than fav.	89	9.7
5. More fav. than unfav.	143	15.6
6. Fairly favorable	95	10.4
7. Quite favorable	74	8.1
8. Very favorable	29	3.2
9. No feelings/don't know	117	12.8
TOTAL	914	100.0

Mean	3.728	Std. err.	0.079
Mode	1.000	Std. dev.	2.226
Kurtosis	-1.281	Skewness	0.166
Median	3.854	Variance	4.955

Range for computation of statistics: 1 through 8.

TABLE III-4(s): GROUP III (Spring, 1973).

Category Label	n	%
1. Very unfavorable	160	16.3
2. Quite unfavorable	79	8.0
3. Fairly unfavorable	91	9.2
4. More unfav. than fav.	125	12.7
5. More fav. than unfav.	171	17.4
6. Fairly favorable	106	10.8
7. Quite favorable	94	9.6
8. Very favorable	41	4.2
9. No feelings/don't know	117	11.9
TOTAL	984	100.0

Mean	4.115	Std. err.	0.072
Mode	5.000	Std. dev.	2.131
Kurtosis	-1.091	Skewness	0.027
Median	4.328	Variance	4.541

Range for computation of statistics: 1 through 8.

Q. 4(t). The military.[43]

TABLE II-4(t):   GROUP II (Fall, 1972).

Category Label	n	%
1. Very unfavorable	152	16.6
2. Quite unfavorable	67	7.3
3. Fairly unfavorable	42	4.6
4. More unfav. than fav.	67	7.3
5. More fav. than unfav.	148	16.2
6. Fairly favorable	122	13.3
7. Quite favorable	144	15.8
8. Very favorable	79	8.6
9. No feelings/don't know	93	10.2
TOTAL	914	100.0

Mean	4.619	Std. err.	0.082
Mode	1.000	Std. dev.	2.358
Kurtosis	-1.228	Skewness	-0.304
Median	5.057	Variance	5.561

Range for computation of statistics: 1 through 8.

TABLE III-4(t):   GROUP III (Spring, 1973).

Category Label	n	%
1. Very unfavorable	169	17.2
2. Quite unfavorable	54	5.5
3. Fairly unfavorable	35	3.6
4. More unfav. than fav.	97	9.9
5. More fav. than unfav.	172	17.5
6. Fairly favorable	145	14.7
7. Quite favorable	136	13.8
8. Very favorable	89	9.0
9. No feelings/don't know	87	8.8
TOTAL	984	100.0

Mean	4.642	Std. err.	0.077
Mode	5.000	Std. dev.	2.315
Kurtosis	-1.110	Skewness	-0.343
Median	5.044	Variance	5.360

Range for computation of statistics: 1 through 8.

FEELINGS TOWARD
POLITICAL FIGURES

Q. 5(a).   George Wallace.[44]

TABLE II-5(a):   GROUP II (Fall, 1972).

Category Label	n	%
1. Very unfavorable	586	64.1
2. Quite unfavorable	113	12.4
3. Fairly unfavorable	47	5.1
4. More unfav. than fav.	53	5.8
5. More fav. than unfav.	37	4.0
6. Fairly favorable	18	2.0
7. Quite favorable	3	0.3
8. Very favorable	1	0.1
9. No feelings/don't know	56	6.1
TOTAL	914	100.0

Mean	1.733	Std. err.	0.045
Mode	1.000	Std. dev.	1.330
Kurtosis	2.864	Skewness	1.913
Median	1.232	Variance	1.769

Range for computation of statistics: 1 through 8.

TABLE III-5(a):   GROUP III (Spring, 1973).

Category Label	n	%
1. Very unfavorable	600	61.0
2. Quite unfavorable	114	11.6
3. Fairly unfavorable	44	4.5
4. More unfav. than fav.	85	8.6
5. More fav. than unfav.	40	4.1
6. Fairly favorable	15	1.5
7. Quite favorable	15	1.5
8. Very favorable	4	0.4
9. No feelings/don't know	67	6.8
TOTAL	984	100.0

Mean	1.883	Std. err.	0.050
Mode	1.000	Std. dev.	1.511
Kurtosis	2.471	Skewness	1.785
Median	1.264	Variance	2.282

Range for computation of statistics: 1 through 8.

Q. 5(b).   Edward Kennedy.[44]

TABLE II-5(b):   GROUP II (Fall, 1972).

Category Label	n	%
1. Very unfavorable	7	0.8
2. Quite unfavorable	3	0.3
3. Fairly unfavorable	4	0.4
4. More unfav. than fav.	11	1.2
5. More fav. than unfav.	82	9.0
6. Fairly favorable	124	13.6
7. Quite favorable	333	36.4
8. Very favorable	305	33.4
9. No feelings/don't know	45	4.9
TOTAL	914	100.0

Mean	6.898	Std. err.	0.041
Mode	7.000	Std. dev.	1.194
Kurtosis	4.640	Skewness	-1.714
Median	7.111	Variance	1.426

Range for computation of statistics: 1 through 8.

TABLE III-5(b):   GROUP III (Spring, 1973).

Category Label	n	%
1. Very unfavorable	7	0.7
2. Quite unfavorable	7	0.7
3. Fairly unfavorable	4	0.4
4. More unfav. than fav.	8	0.8
5. More fav. than unfav.	92	9.3
6. Fairly favorable	184	18.7
7. Quite favorable	383	38.9
8. Very favorable	254	25.8
9. No feelings/don't know	45	4.6
TOTAL	984	100.0

Mean	6.754	Std. err.	0.039
Mode	7.000	Std. dev.	1.183
Kurtosis	4.653	Skewness	-1.638
Median	6.937	Variance	1.399

Range for computation of statistics: 1 through 8.

Q. 5(c). John Ashbrook.[44]

TABLE II-5(c): GROUP II (Fall, 1972).

Category Label	n	%
1. Very unfavorable	46	5.0
2. Quite unfavorable	25	2.7
3. Fairly unfavorable	24	2.6
4. More unfav. than fav.	29	3.2
5. More fav. than unfav.	86	9.4
6. Fairly favorable	66	7.2
7. Quite favorable	41	4.5
8. Very favorable	6	0.7
9. No feelings/don't know	591	64.7
TOTAL	914	100.0

Mean	4.474	Std. err.	0.111
Mode	5.000	Std. dev.	1.994
Kurtosis	-0.897	Skewness	-0.476
Median	4.936	Variance	3.977

Range for computation of statistics: 1 through 8.

TABLE III-5(c): GROUP III (Spring, 1973).

Category Label	n	%
1. Very unfavorable	51	5.2
2. Quite unfavorable	19	1.9
3. Fairly unfavorable	15	1.5
4. More unfav. than fav.	27	2.7
5. More fav. than unfav.	70	7.1
6. Fairly favorable	52	5.3
7. Quite favorable	19	1.9
8. Very favorable	5	0.5
9. No feelings/don't know	726	73.8
TOTAL	984	100.0

Mean	4.174	Std. err.	0.127
Mode	5.000	Std. dev.	2.042
Kurtosis	-1.091	Skewness	-0.360
Median	4.743	Variance	4.168

Range for computation of statistics: 1 through 8.

Q. 5(d). John Connally.[44]

TABLE II-5(d): GROUP II (Fall, 1972).

Category Label	n	%
1. Very unfavorable	75	8.2
2. Quite unfavorable	33	3.6
3. Fairly unfavorable	45	4.9
4. More unfav. than fav.	75	8.2
5. More fav. than unfav.	137	15.0
6. Fairly favorable	97	10.6
7. Quite favorable	46	5.0
8. Very favorable	6	0.7
9. No feelings/don't know	400	43.8
TOTAL	914	100.0

Mean	4.305	Std. err.	0.084
Mode	5.000	Std. dev.	1.893
Kurtosis	-0.817	Skewness	-0.429
Median	4.712	Variance	3.585

Range for computation of statistics: 1 through 8.

TABLE III-5(d): GROUP III (Spring, 1973).

Category Label	n	%
1. Very unfavorable	94	9.6
2. Quite unfavorable	51	5.2
3. Fairly unfavorable	51	5.2
4. More unfav. than fav.	110	11.2
5. More fav. than unfav.	177	18.0
6. Fairly favorable	88	8.9
7. Quite favorable	43	4.4
8. Very favorable	4	0.4
9. No feelings/don't know	366	37.2
TOTAL	984	100.0

Mean	4.102	Std. err.	0.074
Mode	5.000	Std. dev.	1.834
Kurtosis	-0.851	Skewness	-0.351
Median	4.517	Variance	3.362

Range for computation of statistics: 1 through 8.

Q. 5(e). John Lindsay. [44]

TABLE II-5(e): GROUP II (Fall, 1972).

Category Label	n	%
1. Very unfavorable	43	4.7
2. Quite unfavorable	13	1.4
3. Fairly unfavorable	24	2.6
4. More unfav. than fav.	52	5.7
5. More fav. than unfav.	198	21.7
6. Fairly favorable	166	18.2
7. Quite favorable	122	13.3
8. Very favorable	32	3.5
9. No feelings/don't know	264	28.9
TOTAL	914	100.0

Mean	5.300	Std. err.	0.066
Mode	5.000	Std. dev.	1.682
Kurtosis	0.815	Skewness	-0.975
Median	5.475	Variance	2.830

Range for computation of statistics: 1 through 8.

TABLE III-5(e): GROUP III (Spring, 1973).

Category Label	n	%
1. Very unfavorable	39	4.0
2. Quite unfavorable	27	2.7
3. Fairly unfavorable	21	2.1
4. More unfav. than fav.	58	5.9
5. More fav. than unfav.	246	25.0
6. Fairly favorable	168	17.1
7. Quite favorable	106	10.8
8. Very favorable	30	3.0
9. No feelings/don't know	289	29.4
TOTAL	984	100.0

Mean	5.191	Std. err.	0.062
Mode	5.000	Std. dev.	1.631
Kurtosis	0.772	Skewness	-0.894
Median	5.323	Variance	2.659

Range for computation of statistics: 1 through 8.

TABLE II-5(f): GROUP II (Fall, 1972).

Category Label	n	%
1. Very unfavorable	9	1.0
2. Quite unfavorable	4	0.4
3. Fairly unfavorable	4	0.4
4. More unfav. than fav.	10	1.1
5. More fav. than unfav.	33	3.6
6. Fairly favorable	83	9.1
7. Quite favorable	235	25.7
8. Very favorable	513	56.1
9. No feelings/don't know	23	2.5
TOTAL	914	100.0

Mean	7.274	Std. err.	0.040
Mode	8.000	Std. dev.	1.180
Kurtosis	9.036	Skewness	-2.626
Median	7.632	Variance	1.392

Range for computation of statistics: 1 through 8.

TABLE III-5(f): GROUP III (Spring, 1973).

Category Label	n	%
1. Very unfavorable	12	1.2
2. Quite unfavorable	1	0.1
3. Fairly unfavorable	5	0.5
4. More unfav. than fav.	18	1.8
5. More fav. than unfav.	69	7.0
6. Fairly favorable	126	12.8
7. Quite favorable	271	27.5
8. Very favorable	455	46.2
9. No feelings/don't know	27	2.7
TOTAL	984	100.0

Mean	7.042	Std. err.	0.041
Mode	8.000	Std. dev.	1.275
Kurtosis	5.406	Skewness	-1.988
Median	7.413	Variance	1.626

Range for computation of statistics: 1 through 8.

Q. 5(g). Spiro Agnew.[44]

TABLE II-5(g): GROUP II (Fall, 1972).

Category Label	n	%
1. Very unfavorable	292	31.9
2. Quite unfavorable	94	10.3
3. Fairly unfavorable	59	6.5
4. More unfav. than fav.	110	12.0
5. More fav. than unfav.	111	12.1
6. Fairly favorable	83	9.1
7. Quite favorable	34	3.7
8. Very favorable	9	1.0
9. No feelings/don't know	122	13.3
TOTAL	914	100.0

Mean	3.106	Std. err.	0.073
Mode	1.000	Std. dev.	2.050
Kurtosis	-1.124	Skewness	0.448
Median	2.669	Variance	4.201

Range for computation of statistics: 1 through 8.

TABLE III-5(g): GROUP III (Spring, 1973).

Category Label	n	%
1. Very unfavorable	342	34.8
2. Quite unfavorable	103	10.5
3. Fairly unfavorable	74	7.5
4. More unfav. than fav.	146	14.8
5. More fav. than unfav.	103	10.5
6. Fairly favorable	61	6.2
7. Quite favorable	30	3.0
8. Very favorable	5	0.5
9. No feelings/don't know	120	12.2
TOTAL	984	100.0

Mean	2.876	Std. err.	0.065
Mode	1.000	Std. dev.	1.916
Kurtosis	-0.891	Skewness	0.577
Median	2.374	Variance	3.673

Range for computation of statistics: 1 through 8.

FEELINGS TOWARD POLITICAL FIGURES198
Q. 5(h). Wilbur Mills.[44]

TABLE II-5(h): GROUP II (Fall, 1972).

Category Label	n	%
1. Very unfavorable	72	7.9
2. Quite unfavorable	47	5.1
3. Fairly unfavorable	34	3.7
4. More unfav. than fav.	58	6.3
5. More fav. than unfav.	109	11.9
6. Fairly favorable	72	7.9
7. Quite favorable	35	3.8
8. Very favorable	6	0.7
9. No feelings/don't know	481	52.6
TOTAL	914	100.0

Mean	4.088	Std. err.	0.095
Mode	5.000	Std. dev.	1.969
Kurtosis	-1.083	Skewness	-0.237
Median	4.550	Variance	3.877

Range for computation of statistics: 1 through 8.

TABLE III-3(h): GROUP III (Spring, 1973).

Category Label	n	%
1. Very unfavorable	79	8.0
2. Quite unfavorable	39	4.0
3. Fairly unfavorable	19	1.9
4. More unfav. than fav.	53	5.4
5. More fav. than unfav.	110	11.2
6. Fairly favorable	76	7.7
7. Quite favorable	30	3.0
8. Very favorable	5	0.5
9. No feelings/don't know	573	58.2
TOTAL	984	100.0

Mean	4.092	Std. err.	0.099
Mode	5.000	Std. dev.	2.004
Kurtosis	-1.126	Skewness	-0.325
Median	4.641	Variance	4.016

Range for computation of statistics: 1 through 8.

Q. 5(i). Richard Nixon.[44]

TABLE II-5(i): GROUP II (Fall, 1972).

Category Label	n	%
1. Very unfavorable	286	31.3
2. Quite unfavorable	100	10.9
3. Fairly unfavorable	54	5.9
4. More unfav. than fav.	111	12.1
5. More fav. than unfav.	143	15.6
6. Fairly favorable	69	7.5
7. Quite favorable	63	6.9
8. Very favorable	13	1.4
9. No feelings/don't know	75	8.2
TOTAL	914	100.0

Mean	3.297	Std. err.	0.074
Mode	1.000	Std. dev.	2.131
Kurtosis	-1.186	Skewness	0.367
Median	3.120	Variance	4.543

Range for computation of statistics: 1 through 8.

TABLE III-5(i): GROUP III (Spring, 1973).

Category Label	n	%
1. Very unfavorable	413	42.0
2. Quite unfavorable	143	14.5
3. Fairly unfavorable	74	7.5
4. More unfav. than fav.	125	12.7
5. More fav. than unfav.	76	7.7
6. Fairly favorable	48	4.9
7. Quite favorable	26	2.6
8. Very favorable	10	1.0
9. No feelings/don't know	69	7.0
TOTAL	984	100.0

Mean	2.569	Std. err.	0.061
Mode	1.000	Std. dev.	1.857
Kurtosis	-0.143	Skewness	0.964
Median	1.811	Variance	3.449

Range for computation of statistics: 1 through 8.

Q. 5(j). Shirley Chisholm.[44]

TABLE II-5(j): GROUP II (Fall, 1972).

Category Label	n	%
1. Very unfavorable	4	0.4
2. Quite unfavorable	2	0.2
3. Fairly unfavorable	4	0.4
4. More unfav. than fav.	4	0.4
5. More fav. than unfav.	41	4.5
6. Fairly favorable	114	12.5
7. Quite favorable	308	33.7
8. Very favorable	401	43.9
9. No feelings/don't know	36	3.9
TOTAL	914	100.0

Mean	7.163	Std. err.	0.035
Mode	8.000	Std. dev.	1.041
Kurtosis	6.816	Skewness	-2.010
Median	7.377	Variance	1.083

Range for computation of statistics: 1 through 8.

TABLE III-5(j): GROUP III (Spring, 1973).

Category Label	n	%
1. Very unfavorable	5	0.5
2. Quite unfavorable	1	0.1
3. Fairly unfavorable	5	0.5
4. More unfav. than fav.	4	0.4
5. More fav. than unfav.	64	6.5
6. Fairly favorable	120	12.2
7. Quite favorable	373	37.9
8. Very favorable	361	36.7
9. No feelings/don't know	51	5.2
TOTAL	984	100.0

Mean	7.049	Std. err.	0.035
Mode	7.000	Std. dev.	1.064
Kurtosis	5.868	Skewness	-1.834
Median	7.217	Variance	1.133

Range for computation of statistics: 1 through 8.

FEELINGS TOWARD POLITICAL FIGURES
201

Q. 5(k). George McGovern.[44]

TABLE II-5(k): GROUP II (Fall, 1972).

Category Label	n	%
1. Very unfavorable	26	2.8
2. Quite unfavorable	11	1.2
3. Fairly unfavorable	9	1.0
4. More unfav. than fav.	28	3.1
5. More fav. than unfav.	134	14.7
6. Fairly favorable	209	22.9
7. Quite favorable	299	32.7
8. Very favorable	125	13.7
9. No feelings/don't know	73	8.0
TOTAL	914	100.0

Mean	6.188	Std. err.	0.052
Mode	7.000	Std. dev.	1.513
Kurtosis	2.804	Skewness	-1.494
Median	6.512	Variance	2.288

Range for computation of statistics: 1 through 8.

TABLE III-5(k): GROUP III (Spring, 1973).

Category Label	n	%
1. Very unfavorable	24	2.4
2. Quite unfavorable	15	1.5
3. Fairly unfavorable	11	1.1
4. More unfav. than fav.	24	2.4
5. More fav. than unfav.	185	18.8
6. Fairly favorable	268	27.2
7. Quite favorable	297	30.2
8. Very favorable	86	8.7
9. No feelings/don't know	74	7.5
TOTAL	984	100.0

Mean	6.025	Std. err.	0.047
Mode	7.000	Std. dev.	1.431
Kurtosis	2.870	Skewness	-1.424
Median	6.231	Variance	2.047

Range for computation of statistics: 1 through 8.

Q. 5(1). Edmund Muskie.[44]

TABLE II-5(1): GROUP II (Fall, 1972).

Category Label	n	%
1. Very unfavorable	46	5.0
2. Quite unfavorable	14	1.5
3. Fairly unfavorable	17	1.9
4. More unfav. than fav.	50	5.5
5. More fav. than unfav.	187	20.5
6. Fairly favorable	214	23.4
7. Quite favorable	175	19.1
8. Very favorable	50	5.5
9. No feelings/don't know	161	17.6
TOTAL	914	100.0

Mean	5.537	Std. err.	0.061
Mode	6.000	Std. dev.	1.682
Kurtosis	1.208	Skewness	-1.142
Median	5.792	Variance	2.829

Range for computation of statistics: 1 through 8.

TABLE III-5(1): GROUP III (Spring, 1973).

Category Label	n	%
1. Very unfavorable	31	3.2
2. Quite unfavorable	21	2.1
3. Fairly unfavorable	11	1.1
4. More unfav. than fav.	49	5.0
5. More fav. than unfav.	216	22.0
6. Fairly favorable	254	25.8
7. Quite favorable	190	19.3
8. Very favorable	42	4.3
9. No feelings/don't know	170	17.3
TOTAL	984	100.0

Mean	5.617	Std. err.	0.053
Mode	6.000	Std. dev.	1.513
Kurtosis	1.842	Skewness	-1.213
Median	5.811	Variance	2.288

Range for computation of statistics: 1 through 8.

Q. 5(m). Ronald Reagan.[44]

TABLE II-5(m): GROUP II (Fall, 1972).

Category Label	n	%
1. Very unfavorable	153	16.7
2. Quite unfavorable	59	6.5
3. Fairly unfavorable	55	6.0
4. More unfav. than fav.	101	11.1
5. More fav. than unfav.	171	18.7
6. Fairly favorable	103	11.3
7. Quite favorable	42	4.6
8. Very favorable	10	1.1
9. No feelings/don't know	220	24.1
TOTAL	914	100.0

Mean	3.872	Std. err.	0.076
Mode	5.000	Std. dev.	2.002
Kurtosis	-1.161	Skewness	-0.147
Median	4.292	Variance	4.008

Range for computation of statistics: 1 through 8.

TABLE III-5(m): GROUP III (Spring, 1973).

Category Label	n	%
1. Very unfavorable	149	15.1
2. Quite unfavorable	84	8.5
3. Fairly unfavorable	55	5.6
4. More unfav. than fav.	117	11.9
5. More fav. than unfav.	167	17.0
6. Fairly favorable	104	10.6
7. Quite favorable	37	3.8
8. Very favorable	4	0.4
9. No feelings/don't know	267	27.1
TOTAL	984	100.0

Mean	3.766	Std. err.	0.072
Mode	5.000	Std. dev.	1.932
Kurtosis	-1.209	Skewness	-0.118
Median	4.103	Variance	3.733

Range for computation of statistics: 1 through 8.

Q. 5(n). Lester Maddox. [44]

TABLE II-5(n): GROUP II (Fall, 1972).

Category Label	n	%
1. Very unfavorable	323	35.3
2. Quite unfavorable	68	7.4
3. Fairly unfavorable	38	4.2
4. More unfav. than fav.	52	5.7
5. More fav. than unfav.	64	7.0
6. Fairly favorable	61	6.7
7. Quite favorable	22	2.4
8. Very favorable	5	0.5
9. No feelings/don't know	281	30.7
TOTAL	914	100.0

Mean	2.624	Std. err.	0.081
Mode	1.000	Std. dev.	2.030
Kurtosis	-0.703	Skewness	0.863
Median	1.480	Variance	4.121

Range for computation of statistics: 1 through 8.

TABLE III-5(n): GROUP III (Spring, 1973).

Category Label	n	%
1. Very unfavorable	331	33.6
2. Quite unfavorable	73	7.4
3. Fairly unfavorable	44	4.5
4. More unfav. than fav.	57	5.8
5. More fav. than unfav.	66	6.7
6. Fairly favorable	48	4.9
7. Quite favorable	14	1.4
8. Very favorable	3	0.3
9. No feelings/don't know	348	35.4
TOTAL	984	100.0

Mean	2.480	Std. err.	0.075
Mode	1.000	Std. dev.	1.894
Kurtosis	-0.481	Skewness	0.945
Median	1.461	Variance	3.585

Range for computation of statistics: 1 through 8.

FEELINGS TOWARD POLITICAL FIGURES

Q. 5(o).   George Meany. [44]

TABLE II-5(o):   GROUP II (Fall, 1972).

Category Label	n	%
1. Very unfavorable	73	8.0
2. Quite unfavorable	49	5.4
3. Fairly unfavorable	43	4.7
4. More unfav. than fav.	76	8.3
5. More fav. than unfav.	108	11.8
6. Fairly favorable	97	10.6
7. Quite favorable	47	5.1
8. Very favorable	13	1.4
9. No feelings/don't know	408	44.6
TOTAL	914	100.0

Mean	4.267	Std. err.	0.088
Mode	5.000	Std. dev.	1.984
Kurtosis	-0.982	Skewness	-0.259
Median	4.611	Variance	3.935

Range for computation of statistics: 1 through 8.

TABLE III-5(o):   GROUP III (Spring, 1973).

Category Label	n	%
1. Very unfavorable	80	8.1
2. Quite unfavorable	47	4.8
3. Fairly unfavorable	44	4.5
4. More unfav. than fav.	72	7.3
5. More fav. than unfav.	147	14.9
6. Fairly favorable	82	8.3
7. Quite favorable	34	3.5
8. Very favorable	18	1.8
9. No feelings/don't know	460	46.7
TOTAL	984	100.0

Mean	4.204	Std. err.	0.085
Mode	5.000	Std. dev.	1.955
Kurtosis	-0.859	Skewness	-0.240
Median	4.629	Variance	3.822

Range for computation of statistics: 1 through 8.

Q. 5(p). Barry Goldwater.[44]

TABLE II-5(p): GROUP II (Fall, 1972).

Category Label	n	%
1. Very unfavorable	323	35.3
2. Quite unfavorable	102	11.2
3. Fairly unfavorable	62	6.8
4. More unfav. than fav.	117	12.8
5. More fav. than unfav.	85	9.3
6. Fairly favorable	30	3.3
7. Quite favorable	15	1.6
8. Very favorable	1	0.1
9. No feelings/don't know	179	19.6
TOTAL	914	100.0

Mean	2.584	Std. err.	0.065
Mode	1.000	Std. dev.	1.754
Kurtosis	-0.688	Skewness	0.727
Median	1.936	Variance	3.077

Range for computation of statistics: 1 through 8.

TABLE III-5(p): GROUP III (Spring, 1973).

Category Label	n	%
1. Very unfavorable	364	37.0
2. Quite unfavorable	114	11.6
3. Fairly unfavorable	86	8.7
4. More unfav. than fav.	150	15.2
5. More fav. than unfav.	84	8.5
6. Fairly favorable	31	3.2
7. Quite favorable	7	0.7
8. Very favorable	2	0.2
9. No feelings/don't know	146	14.8
TOTAL	984	100.0

Mean	2.531	Std. err.	0.057
Mode	1.000	Std. dev.	1.662
Kurtosis	-0.668	Skewness	0.695
Median	1.982	Variance	2.763

Range for computation of statistics: 1 through 8.

Q. 5(q). Henry Jackson.[44]

TABLE II-5(q): GROUP II (Fall, 1972).

Category Label	n	%
1. Very unfavorable	75	8.2
2. Quite unfavorable	33	3.6
3. Fairly unfavorable	33	3.6
4. More unfav. than fav.	33	3.6
5. More fav. than unfav.	114	12.5
6. Fairly favorable	77	8.4
7. Quite favorable	46	5.0
8. Very favorable	13	1.4
9. No feelings/don't know	490	53.6
TOTAL	914	100.0

Mean	4.316	Std. err.	0.101
Mode	5.000	Std. dev.	2.087
Kurtosis	-1.062	Skewness	-0.332
Median	4.833	Variance	4.354

Range for computation of statistics: 1 through 8.

TABLE III-5(q): GROUP III (Spring, 1973).

Category Label	n	%
1. Very unfavorable	57	5.8
2. Quite unfavorable	26	2.6
3. Fairly unfavorable	21	2.1
4. More unfav. than fav.	50	5.1
5. More fav. than unfav.	97	9.9
6. Fairly favorable	73	7.4
7. Quite favorable	37	3.8
8. Very favorable	11	1.1
9. No feelings/don't know	612	62.2
TOTAL	984	100.0

Mean	4.414	Std. err.	0.103
Mode	5.000	Std. dev.	1.992
Kurtosis	-0.833	Skewness	-0.422
Median	4.830	Variance	3.968

Range for computation of statistics: 1 through 8.

Q. 5(r). Hubert Humphrey.[44]

TABLE II-5(r): GROUP II (Fall, 1972).

Category Label	n	%
1. Very unfavorable	17	1.9
2. Quite unfavorable	18	2.0
3. Fairly unfavorable	13	1.4
4. More unfav. than fav.	36	3.9
5. More fav. than unfav.	171	18.7
6. Fairly favorable	229	25.1
7. Quite favorable	247	27.0
8. Very favorable	88	9.6
9. No feelings/don't know	95	10.4
TOTAL	914	100.0

Mean	5.980	Std. err.	0.051
Mode	7.000	Std. dev.	1.460
Kurtosis	1.963	Skewness	-1.192
Median	6.175	Variance	2.132

Range for computation of statistics: 1 through 8.

TABLE III-5(r): GROUP III (Spring, 1973).

Category Label	n	%
1. Very unfavorable	26	2.6
2. Quite unfavorable	19	1.9
3. Fairly unfavorable	9	0.9
4. More unfav. than fav.	26	2.6
5. More fav. than unfav.	192	19.5
6. Fairly favorable	275	27.9
7. Quite favorable	266	27.0
8. Very favorable	82	8.3
9. No feelings/don't know	89	9.0
TOTAL	984	100.0

Mean	5.947	Std. err.	0.049
Mode	6.000	Std. dev.	1.466
Kurtosis	2.607	Skewness	-1.378
Median	6.138	Variance	2.150

Range for computation of statistics: 1 through 8.

Q. 5(s). Eugene McCarthy.[44]

TABLE II-5(s): GROUP II (Fall, 1972).

Category Label	n	%
1. Very unfavorable	43	4.7
2. Quite unfavorable	28	3.1
3. Fairly unfavorable	17	1.9
4. More unfav. than fav.	53	5.8
5. More fav. than unfav.	238	26.0
6. Fairly favorable	203	22.2
7. Quite favorable	118	12.9
8. Very favorable	24	2.6
9. No feelings/don't know	190	20.8
TOTAL	914	100.0

Mean	5.232	Std. err.	0.060
Mode	5.000	Std. dev.	1.627
Kurtosis	0.956	Skewness	-1.042
Median	5.429	Variance	2.646

Range for computation of statistics: 1 through 8.

TABLE III-5(s): GROUP III (Spring, 1973).

Category Label	n	%
1. Very unfavorable	33	3.4
2. Quite unfavorable	18	1.8
3. Fairly unfavorable	11	1.1
4. More unfav. than fav.	51	5.2
5. More fav. than unfav.	225	22.9
6. Fairly favorable	249	25.3
7. Quite favorable	121	12.3
8. Very favorable	29	2.9
9. No feelings/don't know	247	25.1
TOTAL	984	100.0

Mean	5.433	Std. err.	0.055
Mode	6.000	Std. dev.	1.493
Kurtosis	1.883	Skewness	-1.195
Median	5.622	Variance	2.230

Range for computation of statistics: 1 through 8.

Q. 5(t).   Vance Hartke.[44]

TABLE II-5(t):   GROUP II (Fall, 1972).

Category Label	n	%
1. Very unfavorable	60	6.6
2. Quite unfavorable	40	4.4
3. Fairly unfavorable	17	1.9
4. More unfav. than fav.	47	5.1
5. More fav. than unfav.	72	7.9
6. Fairly favorable	37	4.0
7. Quite favorable	17	1.9
8. Very favorable	3	0.3
9. No feelings/don't know	621	67.9
TOTAL	914	100.0

Mean	3.768	Std. err.	0.115
Mode	5.000	Std. dev.	1.960
Kurtosis	-1.187	Skewness	-0.070
Median	4.128	Variance	3.843

Range for computation of statistics: 1 through 8.

TABLE III-5(t):   GROUP III (Spring, 1973).

Category Label	n	%
1. Very unfavorable	59	6.0
2. Quite unfavorable	21	2.1
3. Fairly unfavorable	12	1.2
4. More unfav. than fav.	33	3.4
5. More fav. than unfav.	77	7.8
6. Fairly favorable	43	4.4
7. Quite favorable	17	1.7
8. Very favorable	2	0.2
9. No feelings/don't know	720	73.2
TOTAL	984	100.0

Mean	3.966	Std. err.	0.124
Mode	5.000	Std. dev.	2.008
Kurtosis	-1.204	Skewness	-0.308
Median	4.591	Variance	4.033

Range for computation of statistics: 1 through 8.

Q. 5(u). Sam Yorty.[44]

TABLE II-5(u): GROUP II (Fall, 1972).

Category Label	n	%
1. Very unfavorable	79	8.6
2. Quite unfavorable	52	5.7
3. Fairly unfavorable	34	3.7
4. More unfav. than fav.	75	8.2
5. More fav. than unfav.	120	13.1
6. Fairly favorable	48	5.3
7. Quite favorable	21	2.3
8. Very favorable	2	0.2
9. No feelings/don't know	483	52.8
TOTAL	914	100.0

Mean	3.796	Std. err.	0.089
Mode	5.000	Std. dev.	1.848
Kurtosis	-1.084	Skewness	-0.177
Median	4.173	Variance	3.414

Range for computation of statistics: 1 through 8.

TABLE III-5(u): GROUP III (Spring, 1973).

Category Label	n	%
1. Very unfavorable	78	7.9
2. Quite unfavorable	36	3.7
3. Fairly unfavorable	21	2.1
4. More unfav. than fav.	70	7.1
5. More fav. than unfav.	123	12.5
6. Fairly favorable	69	7.0
7. Quite favorable	16	1.6
8. Very favorable	3	0.3
9. No feelings/don't know	568	57.7
TOTAL	984	100.0

Mean	3.986	Std. err.	0.092
Mode	5.000	Std. dev.	1.874
Kurtosis	-1.020	Skewness	-0.385
Median	4.524	Variance	3.513

Range for computation of statistics: 1 through 8.

Q. 5(v).   Paul McCloskey.[44]

TABLE II-5(v):   GROUP II (Fall, 1972).

Category Label	n	%
1. Very unfavorable	69	7.5
2. Quite unfavorable	29	3.2
3. Fairly unfavorable	19	2.1
4. More unfav. than fav.	55	6.0
5. More fav. than unfav.	126	13.8
6. Fairly favorable	66	7.2
7. Quite favorable	27	3.0
8. Very favorable	7	0.8
9. No feelings/don't know	516	56.5
TOTAL	914	100.0

Mean	4.209	Std. err.	0.097
Mode	5.000	Std. dev.	1.933
Kurtosis	-0.861	Skewness	-0.424
Median	4.714	Variance	3.737

Range for computation of statistics: 1 through 8.

TABLE III-5(v):   GROUP III (Spring, 1973).

Category Label	n	%
1. Very unfavorable	55	5.6
2. Quite unfavorable	27	2.7
3. Fairly unfavorable	17	1.7
4. More unfav. than fav.	47	4.8
5. More fav. than unfav.	101	10.3
6. Fairly favorable	84	8.5
7. Quite favorable	23	2.3
8. Very favorable	5	0.5
9. No feelings/don't know	625	63.5
TOTAL	984	100.0

Mean	4.340	Std. err.	0.101
Mode	5.000	Std. dev.	1.907
Kurtosis	-0.802	Skewness	-0.542
Median	4.832	Variance	3.638

Range for computation of statistics: 1 through 8.

Q. 5(w).   Terry Sanford.[44]

TABLE II-5(w):   GROUP II (Fall, 1972).

Category Label	n	%
1. Very unfavorable	67	7.3
2. Quite unfavorable	37	4.0
3. Fairly unfavorable	19	2.1
4. More unfav. than fav.	42	4.6
5. More fav. than unfav.	73	8.0
6. Fairly favorable	41	4.5
7. Quite favorable	18	2.0
8. Very favorable	3	0.3
9. No feelings/don't know	614	67.2
TOTAL	914	100.0

Mean	3.757	Std. err.	0.116
Mode	5.000	Std. dev.	2.003
Kurtosis	-1.253	Skewness	-0.069
Median	4.143	Variance	4.011

Range for computation of statistics: 1 through 8.

TABLE III-5(w):   GROUP III (Spring, 1973).

Category Label	n	%
1. Very unfavorable	55	5.6
2. Quite unfavorable	23	2.3
3. Fairly unfavorable	18	1.8
4. More unfav. than fav.	40	4.1
5. More fav. than unfav.	113	11.5
6. Fairly favorable	74	7.5
7. Quite favorable	43	4.4
8. Very favorable	13	1.3
9. No feelings/don't know	605	61.5
TOTAL	984	100.0

Mean	4.562	Std. err.	0.102
Mode	5.000	Std. dev.	1.985
Kurtosis	-0.680	Skewness	-0.530
Median	4.973	Variance	3.940

Range for computation of statistics: 1 through 8.

214
Q. 5(x). William F. Buckley.[44]

TABLE II-5(x): GROUP II (Fall, 1972).

Category Label	n	%
1. Very unfavorable	83	9.1
2. Quite unfavorable	42	4.6
3. Fairly unfavorable	31	3.4
4. More unfav. than fav.	62	6.8
5. More fav. than unfav.	115	12.6
6. Fairly favorable	71	7.8
7. Quite favorable	36	3.9
8. Very favorable	17	1.9
9. No feelings/don't know	457	50.0
TOTAL	914	100.0

Mean	4.151	Std. err.	0.096
Mode	5.000	Std. dev.	2.058
Kurtosis	-1.027	Skewness	-0.187
Median	4.591	Variance	4.234

Range for computation of statistics: 1 through 8.

TABLE III-5(x): GROUP III (Spring, 1973).

Category Label	n	%
1. Very unfavorable	74	7.5
2. Quite unfavorable	52	5.3
3. Fairly unfavorable	33	3.4
4. More unfav. than fav.	70	7.1
5. More fav. than unfav.	123	12.5
6. Fairly favorable	73	7.4
7. Quite favorable	32	3.3
8. Very favorable	13	1.3
9. No feelings/don't know	514	52.2
TOTAL	984	100.0

Mean	4.123	Std. err.	0.091
Mode	5.000	Std. dev.	1.965
Kurtosis	-0.961	Skewness	-0.201
Median	4.549	Variance	3.861

Range for computation of statistics: 1 through 8.

ATTITUDES ON POLICY
TOWARD LABOR UNIONS

LABOR POLICY

Q. 6(a). Unions for postal workers.[45]

TABLE II-6(a): GROUP II (Fall, 1972).

Category Label	n	%
1. Very unfavorable	11	1.2
2. Quite unfavorable	15	1.6
3. Fairly unfavorable	8	0.9
4. More unfav. than fav.	25	2.7
5. More fav. than unfav.	126	13.8
6. Fairly favorable	215	23.5
7. Quite favorable	263	28.8
8. Very favorable	161	17.6
9. No feelings/don't know	90	9.8
TOTAL	914	100.0

Mean	6.328	Std. err.	0.049
Mode	7.000	Std. dev.	1.408
Kurtosis	2.425	Skewness	-1.288
Median	6.546	Variance	1.982

Range for computation of statistics: 1 through 8.

TABLE III-6(a): GROUP III (Spring, 1973).

Category Label	n	%
1. Very unfavorable	13	1.3
2. Quite unfavorable	9	0.9
3. Fairly unfavorable	7	0.7
4. More unfav. than fav.	19	1.9
5. More fav. than unfav.	118	12.0
6. Fairly favorable	211	21.4
7. Quite favorable	322	32.7
8. Very favorable	189	19.2
9. No feelings/don't know	96	9.8
TOTAL	984	100.0

Mean	6.475	Std. err.	0.045
Mode	7.000	Std. dev.	1.345
Kurtosis	3.432	Skewness	-1.488
Median	6.708	Variance	1.808

Range for computation of statistics: 1 through 8.

Q. 6(b).   Unions for firemen.[45]

TABLE II-6(b):   GROUP II (Fall, 1972).

Category Label	n	%
1. Very unfavorable	17	1.9
2. Quite unfavorable	16	1.8
3. Fairly unfavorable	21	2.3
4. More unfav. than fav.	19	2.1
5. More fav. than unfav.	94	10.3
6. Fairly favorable	187	20.5
7. Quite favorable	268	29.3
8. Very favorable	227	24.8
9. No feelings/don't know	65	7.1
TOTAL	914	100.0

Mean	6.445	Std. err.	0.053
Mode	7.000	Std. dev.	1.554
Kurtosis	2.380	Skewness	-1.473
Median	6.763	Variance	2.415

Range for computation of statistics: 1 through 8.

TABLE III-6(b):   GROUP III (Spring, 1973).

Category Label	n	%
1. Very unfavorable	17	1.7
2. Quite unfavorable	12	1.2
3. Fairly unfavorable	5	0.5
4. More unfav. than fav.	21	2.1
5. More fav. than unfav.	96	9.8
6. Fairly favorable	183	18.6
7. Quite favorable	321	32.6
8. Very favorable	249	25.3
9. No feelings/don't know	80	8.1
TOTAL	984	100.0

Mean	6.590	Std. err.	0.048
Mode	7.000	Std. dev.	1.429
Kurtosis	3.720	Skewness	-1.679
Median	6.868	Variance	2.043

Range for computation of statistics: 1 through 8.

Q. 6(c). Unions for phone company workers.[45]

TABLE II-6(c): GROUP II (Fall, 1972).

Category Label	n	%
1. Very unfavorable	14	1.5
2. Quite unfavorable	20	2.2
3. Fairly unfavorable	20	2.2
4. More unfav. than fav.	37	4.0
5. More fav. than unfav.	131	14.3
6. Fairly favorable	211	23.1
7. Quite favorable	237	25.9
8. Very favorable	147	16.1
9. No feelings/don't know	97	10.6
TOTAL	914	100.0

Mean	6.142	Std. err.	0.054
Mode	7.000	Std. dev.	1.541
Kurtosis	1.457	Skewness	-1.143
Median	6.384	Variance	2.374

Range for computation of statistics: 1 through 8.

TABLE III-6(c): GROUP III (Spring, 1973).

Category Label	n	%
1. Very unfavorable	24	2.4
2. Quite unfavorable	13	1.3
3. Fairly unfavorable	12	1.2
4. More unfav. than fav.	36	3.7
5. More fav. than unfav.	124	12.6
6. Fairly favorable	253	25.7
7. Quite favorable	275	27.9
8. Very favorable	145	14.7
9. No feelings/don't know	102	10.4
TOTAL	984	100.0

Mean	6.183	Std. err.	0.051
Mode	7.000	Std. dev.	1.510
Kurtosis	2.516	Skewness	-1.397
Median	6.417	Variance	2.281

Range for computation of statistics: 1 through 8.

Q. 6(d). Unions for general laborers.[45]

TABLE II-6(d): GROUP II (Fall, 1972).

Category Label	n	%
1. Very unfavorable	12	1.3
2. Quite unfavorable	13	1.4
3. Fairly unfavorable	7	0.8
4. More unfav. than fav.	7	0.8
5. More fav. than unfav.	99	10.8
6. Fairly favorable	206	22.5
7. Quite favorable	295	32.3
8. Very favorable	190	20.8
9. No feelings/don't know	85	9.3
TOTAL	914	100.0

Mean	6.517	Std. err.	0.047
Mode	7.000	Std. dev.	1.360
Kurtosis	3.839	Skewness	-1.610
Median	6.739	Variance	1.849

Range for computation of statistics: 1 through 8.

TABLE III-6(d): GROUP III (Spring, 1973).

Category Label	n	%
1. Very unfavorable	6	0.6
2. Quite unfavorable	5	0.5
3. Fairly unfavorable	1	0.1
4. More unfav. than fav.	9	0.9
5. More fav. than unfav.	94	9.6
6. Fairly favorable	225	22.9
7. Quite favorable	348	35.4
8. Very favorable	191	19.4
9. No feelings/don't know	105	10.7
TOTAL	984	100.0

Mean	6.643	Std. err.	0.038
Mode	7.000	Std. dev.	1.128
Kurtosis	4.306	Skewness	-1.408
Median	6.786	Variance	1.273

Range for computation of statistics: 1 through 8.

Q. 6(e). Unions for steel, aircraft workers.[45]

TABLE II-6(e): GROUP II (Fall, 1972).

Category Label	n	%
1. Very unfavorable	9	1.0
2. Quite unfavorable	16	1.8
3. Fairly unfavorable	9	1.0
4. More unfav. than fav.	14	1.5
5. More fav. than unfav.	127	13.9
6. Fairly favorable	204	22.3
7. Quite favorable	250	27.4
8. Very favorable	139	15.2
9. No feelings/don't know	146	16.0
TOTAL	914	100.0

Mean	6.309	Std. err.	0.050
Mode	7.000	Std. dev.	1.388
Kurtosis	2.516	Skewness	-1.297
Median	6.520	Variance	1.927

Range for computation of statistics: 1 through 8.

TABLE III-6(e): GROUP III (Spring, 1973).

Category Label	n	%
1. Very unfavorable	8	0.8
2. Quite unfavorable	13	1.3
3. Fairly unfavorable	10	1.0
4. More unfav. than fav.	18	1.8
5. More fav. than unfav.	127	12.9
6. Fairly favorable	250	25.4
7. Quite favorable	252	25.6
8. Very favorable	139	14.1
9. No feelings/don't know	167	17.0
TOTAL	984	100.0

Mean	6.300	Std. err.	0.046
Mode	7.000	Std. dev.	1.325
Kurtosis	2.587	Skewness	-1.223
Median	6.430	Variance	1.754

Range for computation of statistics: 1 through 8.

Q. 6(f).   Unions for Military Personnel.[45]

TABLE II-6(f):   GROUP II (Fall, 1972).

Category Label	n	%
1. Very unfavorable	61	6.7
2. Quite unfavorable	39	4.3
3. Fairly unfavorable	26	2.8
4. More unfav. than fav.	59	6.5
5. More fav. than unfav.	135	14.8
6. Fairly favorable	164	17.9
7. Quite favorable	189	20.7
8. Very favorable	92	10.1
9. No feelings/don't know	149	16.3
TOTAL	914	100.0

Mean	5.452	Std. err.	0.073
Mode	7.000	Std. dev.	2.008
Kurtosis	-0.128	Skewness	-0.859
Median	5.881	Variance	4.033

Range for computation of statistics: 1 through 8.

TABLE III-6(f):   GROUP III (Spring, 1973).

Category Label	n	%
1. Very unfavorable	72	7.3
2. Quite unfavorable	35	3.6
3. Fairly unfavorable	29	2.9
4. More unfav. than fav.	74	7.5
5. More fav. than unfav.	150	15.2
6. Fairly favorable	194	19.7
7. Quite favorable	198	20.1
8. Very favorable	98	10.0
9. No feelings/don't know	134	13.6
TOTAL	984	100.0

Mean	5.422	Std. err.	0.068
Mode	7.000	Std. dev.	1.993
Kurtosis	-0.074	Skewness	-0.859
Median	5.835	Variance	3.973

Range for computation of statistics: 1 through 8.

Q. 6(g). Unions for school teachers.[45]

TABLE II-6(g): GROUP II (Fall, 1972).

Category Label	n	%
1. Very unfavorable	10	1.1
2. Quite unfavorable	24	2.6
3. Fairly unfavorable	17	1.9
4. More unfav. than fav.	17	1.9
5. More fav. than unfav.	111	12.1
6. Fairly favorable	190	20.8
7. Quite favorable	307	33.6
8. Very favorable	173	18.9
9. No feelings/don't know	65	7.1
TOTAL	914	100.0

Mean	6.366	Std. err.	0.051
Mode	7.000	Std. dev.	1.477
Kurtosis	2.297	Skewness	-1.418
Median	6.681	Variance	2.183

Range for computation of statistics: 1 through 8.

TABLE III-6(g): GROUP III (Spring, 1973).

Category Label	n	%
1. Very unfavorable	12	1.2
2. Quite unfavorable	7	0.7
3. Fairly unfavorable	6	0.6
4. More unfav. than fav.	23	2.3
5. More fav. than unfav.	107	10.9
6. Fairly favorable	206	20.9
7. Quite favorable	358	36.4
8. Very favorable	212	21.5
9. No feelings/don't know	53	5.4
TOTAL	984	100.0

Mean	6.562	Std. err.	0.043
Mode	7.000	Std. dev.	1.302
Kurtosis	3.747	Skewness	-1.543
Median	6.792	Variance	1.696

Range for computation of statistics: 1 through 8.

Q. 6(h). Unions for gas company workers. [45]

TABLE II-6(h): GROUP II (Fall, 1972).

Category Label	n	%
1. Very unfavorable	8	0.9
2. Quite unfavorable	27	3.0
3. Fairly unfavorable	14	1.5
4. More unfav. than fav.	32	3.5
5. More fav. than unfav.	152	16.6
6. Fairly favorable	224	24.5
7. Quite favorable	190	20.8
8. Very favorable	112	12.3
9. No feelings/don't know	155	17.0
TOTAL	914	100.0

Mean	6.011	Std. err.	0.054
Mode	6.000	Std. dev.	1.487
Kurtosis	1.263	Skewness	-0.996
Median	6.154	Variance	2.211

Range for computation of statistics: 1 through 8.

TABLE III-6(h): GROUP III (Spring, 1973).

Category Label	n	%
1. Very unfavorable	14	1.4
2. Quite unfavorable	12	1.2
3. Fairly unfavorable	14	1.4
4. More unfav. than fav.	22	2.2
5. More fav. than unfav.	160	16.3
6. Fairly favorable	247	25.1
7. Quite favorable	231	23.5
8. Very favorable	106	10.8
9. No feelings/don't know	178	18.1
TOTAL	984	100.0

Mean	6.098	Std. err.	0.049
Mode	6.000	Std. dev.	1.394
Kurtosis	2.379	Skewness	-1.200
Median	6.233	Variance	1.942

Range for computation of statistics: 1 through 8.

Q. 6(i).   Unions for building trades workers. [45]

TABLE II-6(i):   GROUP II (Fall, 1972).

Category Label	n	%
1. Very unfavorable	13	1.4
2. Quite unfavorable	16	1.8
3. Fairly unfavorable	10	1.1
4. More unfav. than fav.	25	2.7
5. More fav. than unfav.	137	15.0
6. Fairly favorable	198	21.7
7. Quite favorable	218	23.9
8. Very favorable	139	15.2
9. No feelings/don't know	158	17.3
TOTAL	914	100.0

Mean	6.198	Std. err.	0.054
Mode	7.000	Std. dev.	1.479
Kurtosis	1.960	Skewness	-1.193
Median	6.394	Variance	2.188

Range for computation of statistics: 1 through 8.

TABLE III-6(i):   GROUP III (Spring, 1973).

Category Label	n	%
1. Very unfavorable	9	0.9
2. Quite unfavorable	12	1.2
3. Fairly unfavorable	6	0.6
4. More unfav. than fav.	25	2.5
5. More fav. than unfav.	143	14.5
6. Fairly favorable	254	25.8
7. Quite favorable	245	24.9
8. Very favorable	118	12.0
9. No feelings/don't know	172	17.5
TOTAL	984	100.0

Mean	6 .218	Std. err.	0.046
Mode	6.000	Std. dev.	1.310
Kurtosis	2.570	Skewness	-1.166
Median	6.331	Variance	1.717

Range for computation of statistics: 1 through 8.

Q. 6(j). Unions for dock, warehouse workers. [45]

TABLE II-6(j): GROUP II (Fall, 1972).

Category Label	n	%
1. Very unfavorable	12	1.3
2. Quite unfavorable	16	1.8
3. Fairly unfavorable	8	0.9
4. More unfav. than fav.	24	2.6
5. More fav. than unfav.	147	16.1
6. Fairly favorable	201	22.0
7. Quite favorable	186	20.4
8. Very favorable	109	11.9
9. No feelings/don't know	211	23.1
TOTAL	914	100.0

Mean	6.087	Std. err.	0.055
Mode	6.000	Std. dev.	1.456
Kurtosis	1.908	Skewness	-1.112
Median	6.219	Variance	2.119

Range for computation of statistics: 1 through 8.

TABLE III-6(j): GROUP III (Spring, 1973).

Category Label	n	%
1. Very unfavorable	8	0.8
2. Quite unfavorable	10	1.0
3. Fairly unfavorable	5	0.5
4. More unfav. than fav.	20	2.0
5. More fav. than unfav.	159	16.2
6. Fairly favorable	240	24.4
7. Quite favorable	235	23.9
8. Very favorable	123	12.5
9. No feelings/don't know	184	18.7
TOTAL	984	100.0

Mean	6.234	Std. err.	0.046
Mode	6.000	Std. dev.	1.289
Kurtosis	2.400	Skewness	-1.062
Median	6.325	Variance	1.661

Range for computation of statistics: 1 through 8.

Q. 6(k). Unions for government office workers. [45]

TABLE II-6(k): GROUP II (Fall, 1972).

Category Label	n	%
1. Very unfavorable	45	4.9
2. Quite unfavorable	28	3.1
3. Fairly unfavorable	28	3.1
4. More unfav. than fav.	62	6.8
5. More fav. than unfav.	163	17.8
6. Fairly favorable	197	21.6
7. Quite favorable	177	19.4
8. Very favorable	76	8.3
9. No feelings/don't know	138	15.1
TOTAL	914	100.0

Mean	5.512	Std. err.	0.065
Mode	6.000	Std. dev.	1.807
Kurtosis	0.403	Skewness	-0.928
Median	5.815	Variance	3.267

Range for computation of statistics: 1 through 8.

TABLE III-6(k): GROUP III (Spring, 1973).

Category Label	n	%
1. Very unfavorable	34	3.5
2. Quite unfavorable	26	2.6
3. Fairly unfavorable	19	1.9
4. More unfav. than fav.	56	5.7
5. More fav. than unfav.	183	18.6
6. Fairly favorable	224	22.8
7. Quite favorable	208	21.1
8. Very favorable	94	9.6
9. No feelings/don't know	140	14.2
TOTAL	984	100.0

Mean	5.727	Std. err.	0.058
Mode	6.000	Std. dev.	1.675
Kurtosis	1.017	Skewness	-1.047
Median	5.964	Variance	2.806

Range for computation of statistics: 1 through 8.

Q. 6(1). Unions for policemen. [45]

TABLE II-6(1): GROUP II (Fall, 1972).

Category Label	n	%
1. Very unfavorable	123	13.5
2. Quite unfavorable	59	6.5
3. Fairly unfavorable	30	3.3
4. More unfav. than fav.	90	9.8
5. More fav. than unfav.	128	14.0
6. Fairly favorable	149	16.3
7. Quite favorable	151	16.5
8. Very favorable	93	10.2
9. No feelings/don't know	91	10.0
TOTAL	914	100.0

Mean	4.892	Std. err.	0.080
Mode	7.000	Std. dev.	2.284
Kurtosis	−1.004	Skewness	−0.463
Median	5.355	Variance	5.218

Range for computation of statistics: 1 through 8.

TABLE III-6(1): GROUP III (Spring, 1973).

Category Label	n	%
1. Very unfavorable	130	13.2
2. Quite unfavorable	51	5.2
3. Fairly unfavorable	34	3.5
4. More unfav. than fav.	104	10.6
5. More fav. than unfav.	176	17.9
6. Fairly favorable	156	15.9
7. Quite favorable	159	16.2
8. Very favorable	77	7.8
9. No feelings/don't know	97	9.9
TOTAL	984	100.0

Mean	4.842	Std. err.	0.073
Mode	5.000	Std. dev.	2.188
Kurtosis	−0.859	Skewness	−0.491
Median	5.207	Variance	4.788

Range for computation of statistics: 1 through 8.

Q. 6(m). Unions for electric company workers.[45]

TABLE II-6(m): GROUP II (Fall, 1972).

Category Label	n	%
1. Very unfavorable	14	1.5
2. Quite unfavorable	27	3.0
3. Fairly unfavorable	20	2.2
4. More unfav. than fav.	26	2.8
5. More fav. than unfav.	149	16.3
6. Fairly favorable	194	21.2
7. Quite favorable	200	21.9
8. Very favorable	145	15.9
9. No feelings/don't know	139	15.2
TOTAL	914	100.0

Mean	6.066	Std. err	0.058
Mode	7.000	Std. dev.	1.604
Kurtosis	1.139	Skewness	-1.067
Median	6.281	Variance	2.573

Range for computation of statistics: 1 through 8.

TABLE III-6(m): GROUP III (Spring, 1973).

Category Label	n	%
1. Very unfavorable	18	1.8
2. Quite unfavorable	9	0.9
3. Fairly unfavorable	13	1.3
4. More unfav. than fav.	24	2.4
5. More fav. than unfav.	152	15.4
6. Fairly favorable	244	24.8
7. Quite favorable	240	24.4
8. Very favorable	130	13.2
9. No feelings/don't know	154	15.7
TOTAL	984	100.0

Mean	6.163	Std. err.	0.050
Mode	6.000	Std. dev.	1.431
Kurtosis	2.524	Skewness	-1.265
Median	6.316	Variance	2.047

Range for computation of statistics: 1 through 8.

Q. 6(n). Unions for farm laborers.[45]

TABLE II-6(n): GROUP II (Fall, 1972).

Category Label	n	%
1. Very unfavorable	20	2.2
2. Quite unfavorable	15	1.6
3. Fairly unfavorable	13	1.4
4. More unfav. than fav.	26	2.8
5. More fav. than unfav.	107	11.7
6. Fairly favorable	173	18.9
7. Quite favorable	264	28.9
8. Very favorable	194	21.2
9. No feelings/don't know	102	11.2
TOTAL	914	100.0

Mean	6.362	Std. err.	0.055
Mode	7.000	Std. dev.	1.571
Kurtosis	2.313	Skewness	-1.438
Median	6.697	Variance	2.468

Range for computation of statistics: 1 through 8.

TABLE III-6(n): GROUP III (Spring, 1973).

Category Label	n	%
1. Very unfavorable	13	1.3
2. Quite unfavorable	8	0.8
3. Fairly unfavorable	11	1.1
4. More unfav. than fav.	17	1.7
5. More fav. than unfav.	122	12.4
6. Fairly favorable	183	18.6
7. Quite favorable	295	30.0
8. Very favorable	216	22.0
9. No feelings/don't know	119	12.1
TOTAL	984	100.0

Mean	6.510	Std. err.	0.047
Mode	7.000	Std. dev.	1.393
Kurtosis	2.954	Skewness	-1.434
Median	6.766	Variance	1.940

Range for computation of statistics: 1 through 8.

Q. 6(o). Unions for truck drivers, teamsters. [45]

TABLE II-6(o): GROUP II (Fall, 1972).

Category Label	n	%
1. Very unfavorable	13	1.4
2. Quite unfavorable	16	1.8
3. Fairly unfavorable	15	1.6
4. More unfav. than fav.	30	3.3
5. More fav. than unfav.	136	14.9
6. Fairly favorable	232	25.4
7. Quite favorable	216	23.6
8. Very favorable	109	11.9
9. No feelings/don't know	147	16.1
TOTAL	914	100.0

Mean	6.083	Std. err.	0.052
Mode	6.000	Std. dev.	1.454
Kurtosis	1.930	Skewness	-1.168
Median	6.248	Variance	2.113

Range for computation of statistics: 1 through 8.

TABLE III-6(o): GROUP III (Spring, 1973).

Category Label	n	%
1. Very unfavorable	12	1.2
2. Quite unfavorable	12	1.2
3. Fairly unfavorable	9	0.9
4. More unfav. than fav.	26	2.6
5. More fav. than unfav.	139	14.1
6. Fairly favorable	263	26.7
7. Quite favorable	241	24.5
8. Very favorable	133	13.5
9. No feelings/don't know	149	15.1
TOTAL	984	100.0

Mean	6.217	Std. err	0.047
Mode	6.000	Std. dev.	1.363
Kurtosis	2.561	Skewness	-1.216
Median	6.335	Variance	1.858

Range for computation of statistics: 1 through 8.

Q. 6(p). Unions for garbage workers.[45]

TABLE II-6(p): GROUP II (Fall, 1972).

Category Label	n	%
1. Very unfavorable	18	2.0
2. Quite unfavorable	28	3.1
3. Fairly unfavorable	17	1.9
4. More unfav. than fav.	29	3.2
5. More fav. than unfav.	120	13.1
6. Fairly favorable	189	20.7
7. Quite favorable	239	26.1
8. Very favorable	187	20.5
9. No feelings/don't know	87	9.5
TOTAL	914	100.0

Mean	6.220	Std. err.	0.057
Mode	7.000	Std. dev.	1.645
Kurtosis	1.470	Skewness	-1.253
Median	6.552	Variance	2.705

Range for computation of statistics: 1 through 8.

TABLE III-6(p): GROUP III (Spring, 1973).

Category Label	n	%
1. Very unfavorable	21	2.1
2. Quite unfavorable	9	0.9
3. Fairly unfavorable	11	1.1
4. More unfav. than fav.	24	2.4
5. More fav. than unfav.	121	12.3
6. Fairly favorable	210	21.3
7. Quite favorable	269	27.3
8. Very favorable	223	22.7
9. No feelings/don't know	96	9.8
TOTAL	984	100.0

Mean	6.419	Std. err.	0.050
Mode	7.000	Std. dev.	1.498
Kurtosis	2.775	Skewness	-1.451
Median	6.678	Variance	2.244

Range for computation of statistics: 1 through 8.

Q. 6(q). Unions for coal mine workers.[45]

TABLE II-6(q): GROUP II (Fall, 1972).

Category Label	n	%
1. Very unfavorable	21	2.3
2. Quite unfavorable	21	2.3
3. Fairly unfavorable	19	2.1
4. More unfav. than fav.	24	2.6
5. More fav. than unfav.	119	13.0
6. Fairly favorable	183	20.0
7. Quite favorable	212	23.2
8. Very favorable	143	15.6
9. No feelings/don't know	172	18.8
TOTAL	914	100.0

Mean	6.115	Std. err.	0.061
Mode	7.000	Std. dev.	1.652
Kurtosis	1.494	Skewness	-1.238
Median	6.413	Variance	2.728

Range for computation of statistics: 1 through 8.

TABLE III-6(q): GROUP III (Spring, 1973).

Category Label	n	%
1. Very unfavorable	18	1.8
2. Quite unfavorable	12	1.2
3. Fairly unfavorable	10	1.0
4. More unfav. than fav.	23	2.3
5. More fav. than unfav.	113	11.5
6. Fairly favorable	201	20.4
7. Quite favorable	223	22.7
8. Very favorable	175	17.8
9. No feelings/don't know	209	21.2
TOTAL	984	100.0

Mean	6.317	Std. err.	0.055
Mode	7.000	Std. dev.	1.517
Kurtosis	2.418	Skewness	-1.362
Median	6.547	Variance	2.302

Range for computation of statistics: 1 through 8.

Q. 6(r). Unions for college professors.[45]

TABLE II-6(r): GROUP II (Fall, 1972).

Category Label	n	%
1. Very unfavorable	22	2.4
2. Quite unfavorable	18	2.0
3. Fairly unfavorable	22	2.4
4. More unfav. than fav.	24	2.6
5. More fav. than unfav.	121	13.2
6. Fairly favorable	209	22.9
7. Quite favorable	269	29.4
8. Very favorable	143	15.6
9. No feelings/don't know	86	9.4
TOTAL	914	100.0

Mean	6.167	Std. err.	0.055
Mode	7.000	Std. dev.	1.582
Kurtosis	1.977	Skewness	-1.353
Median	6.490	Variance	2.504

Range for computation of statistics: 1 through 8.

TABLE III-6(r): GROUP III (Spring, 1973).

Category Label	n	%
1. Very unfavorable	19	1.9
2. Quite unfavorable	11	1.1
3. Fairly unfavorable	20	2.0
4. More unfav. than fav.	32	3.3
5. More fav. than unfav.	134	13.6
6. Fairly favorable	235	23.9
7. Quite favorable	299	30.4
8. Very favorable	149	15.1
9. No feelings/don't know	85	8.6
TOTAL	984	100.0

Mean	6.222	Std. err.	0.049
Mode	7.000	Std. dev.	1.471
Kurtosis	2.341	Skewness	-1.338
Median	6.494	Variance	2.164

Range for computation of statistics: 1 through 8.

Q. 8(a). Right to unionize: steel and aircraft. [50]

TABLE II-8(a): GROUP II (Fall, 1972).

Category Label	n	%
0. No response	18	2.0
1. Agree a lot	520	56.9
2. Agree a little	310	33.9
3. Disagree a little	47	5.1
4. Disagree a lot	19	2.1
TOTAL	914	100.0

Mean	1.485	Std. err.	0.024
Mode	1.000	Std. dev.	0.719
Kurtosis	1.692	Skewness	1.149
Median	1.344	Variance	0.517

Range for computation of statistics: 1 through 4.

TABLE III-8(a): GROUP III (Spring, 1973).

Category Label	n	%
0. No response	7	0.7
1. Agree a lot	530	53.9
2. Agree a little	384	39.0
3. Disagree a little	50	5.1
4. Disagree a lot	13	1.3
TOTAL	984	100.0

Mean	1.524	Std. err.	0.021
Mode	1.000	Std. dev.	0.667
Kurtosis	1.228	Skewness	1.021
Median	1.415	Variance	0.445

Range for computation of statistics: 1 through 4.

Q. 8(b). Right to unionize: phone, gas, electric.[51]

TABLE II-8(b): GROUP II (Fall, 1972).

Category Label	n	%
0. No response	20	2.2
1. Agree a lot	468	51.2
2. Agree a little	324	35.4
3. Disagree a little	77	8.4
4. Disagree a lot	25	2.7
TOTAL	914	100.0

Mean	1.583	Std. err.	0.026
Mode	1.000	Std. dev.	0.787
Kurtosis	0.853	Skewness	0.949
Median	1.434	Variance	0.620

Range for computation of statistics: 1 through 4.

TABLE III-8(b): GROUP III (Spring, 1973).

Category Label	n	%
0. No response	7	0.7
1. Agree a lot	511	51.9
2. Agree a little	353	35.9
3. Disagree a little	84	8.5
4. Disagree a lot	29	2.9
TOTAL	984	100.0

Mean	1.611	Std. err.	0.025
Mode	1.000	Std. dev.	0.775
Kurtosis	0.910	Skewness	1.085
Median	1.449	Variance	0.600

Range for computation of statistics: 1 through 4.

Q. 8(c).   Should not let unions have much say. [52]

TABLE II-8(c): GROUP II (Fall, 1972).

Category Label		n	%
0. No response		22	2.4
1. Agree a lot		125	13.7
2. Agree a little		186	20.4
3. Disagree a little		303	33.2
4. Disagree a lot		278	30.4
TOTAL		914	100.0
Mean	2.755	Std. err.	0.036
Mode	3.000	Std. dev.	1.101
Kurtosis	-0.629	Skewness	-0.553
Median	2.909	Variance	1.213

Range for computation of statistics: 1 through 4.

TABLE III-8(c): GROUP III (Spring, 1973).

Catagory Label		n	%
0. No response		13	1.3
1. Agree a lot		84	8.5
2. Agree a little		192	19.5
3. Disagree a little		330	33.5
4. Disagree a lot		365	37.1
TOTAL		984	100.0
Mean	2.965	Std. err.	0.032
Mode	4.000	Std. dev.	1.013
Kurtosis	-0.253	Skewness	-0.729
Median	3.115	Variance	1.026

Range for computation of statistics: 1 through 4.

Q. 8(d). Right to unionize: Goverment office workers.[53]

TABLE II-8(d): GROUP II (Fall, 1972).

Category Label	n	%
0. No response	23	2.5
1. Agree a lot	242	26.5
2. Agree a little	305	33.4
3. Disagree a little	204	22.3
4. Disagree a lot	140	15.3
TOTAL	914	100.0

Mean	2.214	Std. err.	0.036
Mode	2.000	Std. dev.	1.075
Kurtosis	-0.887	Skewness	0.185
Median	2.130	Variance	1.157

Range for computation of statistics: 1 through 4.

TABLE III-8(d): GROUP III (Spring, 1973).

Category Label	n	%
0. No response	13	1.3
1. Agree a lot	278	28.3
2. Agree a little	360	36.6
3. Disagree a little	190	19.3
4. Disagree a lot	143	14.5
TOTAL	984	100.0

Mean	2.175	Std. err.	0.033
Mode	2.000	Std. dev.	1.039
Kurtosis	-0.824	Skewness	0.353
Median	2.058	Variance	1.080

Range for computation of statistics: 1 through 4.

Q. 8(e). Right to unionize: teachers. [54]

TABLE II-8(e): GROUP II (Fall, 1972).

Category Label	n	%
0. No response	28	3.1
1. Agree a lot	434	47.5
2. Agree a little	321	35.1
3. Disagree a little	84	9.2
4. Disagree a lot	47	5.1
TOTAL	914	100.0

Mean	1.659	Std. err.	0.029
Mode	1.000	Std. dev.	0.883
Kurtosis	0.575	Skewness	0.903
Median	1.488	Variance	0.779

Range for computation of statistics: 1 through 4.

TABLE III-8(e): GROUP III (Spring, 1973).

Category Label	n	%
0. No response	11	1.1
1. Agree a lot	538	54.7
2. Agree a little	319	32.4
3. Disagree a little	79	8.0
4. Disagree a lot	37	3.8
TOTAL	984	100.0

Mean	1.586	Std. err.	0.026
Mode	1.000	Std. dev.	0.807
Kurtosis	1.104	Skewness	1.186
Median	1.394	Variance	0.652

Range for computation of statistics: 1 through 4.

Q. 8(f).   Unions should have more influence. [55]

TABLE II-8(f):   GROUP II (Fall, 1972).

Category Label	n	%
0. No response	24	2.6
1. Agree a lot	79	8.6
2. Agree a little	192	21.0
3. Disagree a little	317	34.7
4. Disagree a lot	302	33.0
TOTAL	914	100.0

Mean	2.869	Std. err.	0.035
Mode	3.000	Std. dev.	1.052
Kurtosis	−0.144	Skewness	−0.725
Median	3.011	Variance	1.107

Range for computation of statistics: 1 through 4.

TABLE III-8(f):   GROUP III (Spring, 1973).

Category Label	n	%
0. No response	12	1.2
1. Agree a lot	59	6.0
2. Agree a little	226	23.0
3. Disagree a little	370	37.6
4. Disagree a lot	317	32.2
TOTAL	984	100.0

Mean	2.936	Std. err.	0.030
Mode	3.000	Std. dev.	0.948
Kurtosis	−0.100	Skewness	−0.639
Median	3.027	Variance	0.898

Range for computation of statistics: 1 through 4.

Q. 8(g). Right to unionize: firemen, policemen.[56]

TABLE II-8(g): GROUP II (Fall, 1972).

Category Label	n	%
0. No response	25	2.7
1. Agree a lot	316	34.6
2. Agree a little	310	33.9
3. Disagree a little	165	18.1
4. Disagree a lot	98	10.7
TOTAL	914	100.0

Mean	1.995	Std. err.	0.034
Mode	1.000	Std. dev.	1.032
Kurtosis	-0.629	Skewness	0.447
Median	1.874	Variance	1.066

Range for computation of statistics: 1 through 4.

TABLE III-8(g): GROUP III (Spring, 1973).

Category Label	n	%
0. No response	14	1.4
1. Agree a lot	334	33.9
2. Agree a little	389	39.5
3. Disagree a little	144	14.6
4. Disagree a lot	103	10.5
TOTAL	984	100.0

Mean	1.988	Std. err.	0.031
Mode	2.000	Std. dev.	0.981
Kurtosis	-0.389	Skewness	0.600
Median	1.870	Variance	0.962

Range for computation of statistics: 1 through 4.

Q. 8(h). Right to unionize: general laborers.[57]

TABLE II-8(h): GROUP II (Fall, 1972).

Category Label	n	%
0. No response	23	2.5
1. Agree a lot	518	56.7
2. Agree a little	305	33.4
3. Disagree a little	53	5.8
4. Disagree a lot	15	1.6
TOTAL	914	100.0

Mean	1.474	Std. err.	0.024
Mode	1.000	Std. dev.	0.717
Kurtosis	1.369	Skewness	1.027
Median	1.338	Variance	0.515

Range for computation of statistics: 1 through 4.

TABLE III-8(h): GROUP III (Spring, 1973).

Category Label	n	%
0. No response	10	1.0
1. Agree a lot	588	59.8
2. Agree a little	330	33.5
3. Disagree a little	44	4.5
4. Disagree a lot	12	1.2
TOTAL	984	100.0

Mean	1.451	Std. err.	0.021
Mode	1.000	Std. dev.	0.656
Kurtosis	1.700	Skewness	1.194
Median	1.320	Variance	0.431

Range for computation of statistics: 1 through 4.

LABOR POLICY

Q. 8(i). Right to unionize: garbage workers.[58]

TABLE II-8(i): GROUP II (Fall, 1972).

Category Label	n	%
0. No response	21	2.3
1. Agree a lot	551	60.3
2. Agree a little	256	28.0
3. Disagree a little	56	6.1
4. Disagree a lot	30	3.3
TOTAL	914	100.0

Mean	1.478	Std. err.	0.026
Mode	1.000	Std. dev.	0.785
Kurtosis	1.803	Skewness	1.331
Median	1.291	Variance	0.616

Range for computation of statistics: 1 through 4.

TABLE III-8(i): GROUP III (Spring, 1973).

Category Label	n	%
0. No response	9	0.9
1. Agree a lot	593	60.3
2. Agree a little	306	31.1
3. Disagree a little	50	5.1
4. Disagree a lot	26	2.6
TOTAL	984	100.0

Mean	1.483	Std. err.	0.023
Mode	1.000	Std. dev.	0.727
Kurtosis	2.119	Skewness	1.418
Median	1.315	Variance	0.529

Range for computation of statistics: 1 through 4.

Q. 8(j). Laws limiting unions are necessary.[59]

TABLE II-8(j): GROUP II (Fall, 1972).

Category Label	n	%
0. No response	7	0.8
1. Agree a lot	389	42.6
2. Agree a little	381	41.7
3. Disagree a little	98	10.7
4. Disagree a lot	39	4.3
TOTAL	914	100.0

Mean	1.752	Std. err.	0.027
Mode	1.000	Std. dev.	0.820
Kurtosis	0.447	Skewness	0.866
Median	1.660	Variance	0.673

Range for computation of statistics: 1 through 4.

TABLE III-8(j): GROUP III (Spring, 1973).

Category Label	n	%
0. No response	27	2.7
1. Agree a lot	404	41.1
2. Agree a little	425	43.2
3. Disagree a little	97	9.9
4. Disagree a lot	31	3.2
TOTAL	984	100.0

Mean	1.696	Std. err.	0.026
Mode	2.000	Std. dev.	0.808
Kurtosis	0.518	Skewness	0.651
Median	1.644	Variance	0.653

Range for computation of statistics: 1 through 4.

Q. 8(k). Right to unionize: post office workers. [60]

TABLE II-8(k): GROUP II (Fall, 1972).

Category Label		n	%
0.	No response	9	1.0
1.	Agree a lot	382	41.8
2.	Agree a little	357	39.1
3.	Disagree a little	119	13.0
4.	Disagree a lot	47	5.1
TOTAL		914	100.0

Mean	1.795	Std. err.	0.029
Mode	1.000	Std. dev.	0.867
Kurtosis	0.113	Skewness	0.790
Median	1.685	Variance	0.752

Range for computation of statistics: 1 through 4.

TABLE III-8(k): GROUP III (Spring, 1973).

Category Label		n	%
0.	No response	27	2.7
1.	Agree a lot	435	44.2
2.	Agree a little	383	38.9
3.	Disagree a little	100	10.2
4.	Disagree a lot	39	4.0
TOTAL		984	100.0

Mean	1.684	Std. err.	0.027
Mode	1.000	Std. dev.	0.844
Kurtosis	0.480	Skewness	0.772
Median	1.578	Variance	0.713

Range for computation of statistics: 1 through 4.

Q. 8(1). Right to unionize: military personnel.[61]

TABLE II-8(1): GROUP II (Fall, 1972).

Category Label	n	%
0. No response	17	1.9
1. Agree a lot	232	25.4
2. Agree a little	241	26.4
3. Disagree a little	245	26.8
4. Disagree a lot	179	19.6
TOTAL	914	100.0

Mean	2.369	Std. err.	0.037
Mode	3.000	Std. dev.	1.116
Kurtosis	-1.120	Skewness	0.005
Median	2.363	Variance	1.245

Range for computation of statistics: 1 through 4.

TABLE III-8(1): GROUP III (Spring, 1973).

Category Label	n	%
0. No response	31	3.2
1. Agree a lot	230	23.4
2. Agree a little	257	26.1
3. Disagree a little	241	24.5
4. Disagree a lot	225	22.9
TOTAL	984	100.0

Mean	2.405	Std. err.	0.037
Mode	2.000	Std. dev.	1.165
Kurtosis	-1.105	Skewness	-0.080
Median	2.399	Variance	1.356

Range for computation of statistics: 1 through 4.

Q. 8(m). Unions necessary to protect working man.[62]

TABLE II-8(m): GROUP II (Fall, 1972).

Category Label		n	%
0.	No response	9	1.0
1.	Agree a lot	10	1.1
2.	Agree a little	52	5.7
3.	Disagree a little	272	29.8
4.	Disagree a lot	571	62.5
TOTAL		914	100.0

Mean	3.516	Std. err.	0.024
Mode	4.000	Std. dev.	0.740
Kurtosis	4.671	Skewness	-1.904
Median	3.700	Variance	0.548

Range for computation of statistics: 1 through 4.

TABLE III-8(m): GROUP III (Spring, 1973).

Category Label		n	%
0.	No response	25	2.5
1.	Agree a lot	15	1.5
2.	Agree a little	43	4.4
3.	Disagree a little	245	24.9
4.	Disagree a lot	656	66.7
TOTAL		984	100.0

Mean	3.516	Std. err.	0.027
Mode	4.000	Std. dev.	0.857
Kurtosis	5.876	Skewness	-2.321
Median	3.750	Variance	0.734

Range for computation of statistics: 1 through 4.

Q. 8(n). Right to strike: steel, aircraft worker. [63]

TABLE II-8(n): GROUP II (Fall, 1972).

Category Label	n	%
0. No response	10	1.1
1. Agree a lot	453	49.6
2. Agree a little	333	36.4
3. Disagree a little	96	10.5
4. Disagree a lot	22	2.4
TOTAL	914	100.0

Mean	1.636	Std. err.	0.026
Mode	1.000	Std. dev.	0.780
Kurtosis	0.464	Skewness	0.901
Median	1.487	Variance	0.609

Range for computation of statistics: 1 through 4.

TABLE III-8(n): GROUP III (Spring, 1972).

Category Label	n	%
0. No response	25	2.5
1. Agree a lot	482	49.0
2. Agree a little	355	36.1
3. Disagree a little	100	10.2
4. Disagree a lot	22	2.2
TOTAL	984	100.0

Mean	1.606	Std. err.	0.025
Mode	1.000	Std. dev.	0.792
Kurtosis	0.462	Skewness	0.786
Median	1.469	Variance	0.628

Range for computation of statistics: 1 through 4.

Q. 8(o). Right to strike: phone, gas, electric.[64]

TABLE II-8(o): GROUP II (Fall, 1972).

Category Label	n	%
0. No response	16	1.8
1. Agree a lot	383	41.9
2. Agree a little	307	33.6
3. Disagree a little	152	16.6
4. Disagree a lot	56	6.1
TOTAL	914	100.0

Mean	1.835	Std. err.	0.031
Mode	1.000	Std. dev.	0.935
Kurtosis	-0.307	Skewness	0.655
Median	1.689	Variance	0.874

Range for computation of statistics: 1 through 4.

TABLE III-8(o): GROUP III (Spring, 1973).

Category Label	n	%
0. No response	22	2.2
1. Agree a lot	410	41.7
2. Agree a little	331	33.6
3. Disagree a little	150	15.2
4. Disagree a lot	71	7.2
TOTAL	984	100.0

Mean	1.835	Std. err.	0.031
Mode	1.000	Std. dev.	0.960
Kurtosis	-0.260	Skewness	0.672
Median	1.681	Variance	0.921

Range for computation of statistics: 1 through 4.

Q. 8(p).   Government should regulate unions more.[65]

TABLE II-8(p):   GROUP II (Fall, 1972).

Category Label	n	%
0. No response	12	1.3
1. Agree a lot	245	26.8
2. Agree a little	337	36.9
3. Disagree a little	223	24.4
4. Disagree a lot	97	10.6
TOTAL	914	100.0

Mean	2.162	Std. err.	0.032
Mode	2.000	Std. dev.	0.982
Kurtosis	-0.729	Skewness	0.262
Median	2.093	Variance	0.964

Range for computation of statistics: 1 through 4.

TABLE III-8(p):   GROUP III (Spring, 1973).

Category Label	n	%
0. No response	28	2.8
1. Agree a lot	202	20.5
2. Agree a little	316	32.1
3. Disagree a little	300	30.5
4. Disagree a lot	138	14.0
TOTAL	914	100.0

Mean	2.323	Std. err.	0.033
Mode	2.000	Std. dev.	1.040
Kurtosis	-0.746	Skewness	-0.078
Median	2.329	Variance	1.082

Range for computation of statistics: 1 through 4.

Q. 8(q). Right to strike: government office workers.[66]

TABLE II-8(q): GROUP II (Fall, 1972).

Category Label	n	%
0. No response	10	1.1
1. Agree a lot	272	29.8
2. Agree a little	263	28.8
3. Disagree a little	210	23.0
4. Disagree a lot	159	17.4
TOTAL	914	100.0

Mean	2.258	Std. err.	0.036
Mode	1.000	Std. dev.	1.096
Kurtosis	-1.126	Skewness	0.220
Median	2.165	Variance	1.202

Range for computation of statistics: 1 through 4.

TABLE III-8(q): GROUP III (Spring, 1973).

Category Label	n	%
0. No response	26	2.6
1. Agree a lot	277	28.2
2. Agree a little	313	31.8
3. Disagree a little	226	23.0
4. Disagree a lot	142	14.4
TOTAL	984	100.0

Mean	2.184	Std. err.	0.034
Mode	2.000	Std. dev.	1.078
Kurtosis	-0.903	Skewness	0.196
Median	2.104	Variance	1.161

Range for computation of statistics: 1 through 4.

Q. 8(r). Right to strike: teachers. [67]

TABLE II-8(r): GROUP II (Fall, 1972).

Category Label	n	%
0. No response	14	1.5
1. Agree a lot	456	49.9
2. Agree a little	304	33.3
3. Disagree a little	91	10.0
4. Disagree a lot	49	5.4
TOTAL	914	100.0

Mean	1.677	Std. err.	0.029
Mode	1.000	Std. dev.	0.878
Kurtosis	0.530	Skewness	1.015
Median	1.471	Variance	0.771

Range for computation of statistics: 1 through 4.

TABLE III-8(r): GROUP III (Spring, 1973).

Category Label	n	%
0. No response	24	2.4
1. Agree a lot	501	50.9
2. Agree a little	327	33.2
3. Disagree a little	82	8.3
4. Disagree a lot	50	5.1
TOTAL	984	100.0

Mean	1.627	Std. err.	0.028
Mode	1.000	Std. dev.	0.869
Kurtosis	0.799	Skewness	1.040
Median	1.434	Variance	0.755

Range for computation of statistics: 1 through 4.

Q. 8(s). Should not have to join union for job. [68]

TABLE II-8(s): GROUP II (Fall, 1972).

Category Label	n	%
0. No response	12	1.3
1. Agree a lot	537	58.8
2. Agree a little	199	21.8
3. Disagree a little	94	10.3
4. Disagree a lot	72	7.9
TOTAL	914	100.0

Mean	1.647	Std. err.	0.032
Mode	1.000	Std. dev.	0.967
Kurtosis	0.401	Skewness	1.191
Median	1.329	Variance	0.934

Range for computation of statistics: 1 through 4.

TABLE III-8(s): GROUP III (Spring, 1973).

Category Label	n	%
0. No response	23	2.3
1. Agree a lot	591	60.1
2. Agree a little	223	22.7
3. Disagree a little	80	8.1
4. Disagree a lot	67	6.8
TOTAL	984	100.0

Mean	1.570	Std. err.	0.030
Mode	1.000	Std. dev.	0.929
Kurtosis	0.926	Skewness	1.285
Median	1.294	Variance	0.864

Range for computation of statistics: 1 through 4.

Q. 8(t). Right to strike: firemen and policemen. [69]

TABLE II-8(t): GROUP II (Fall, 1972).

Category Label	n	%
0. No response	8	0.9
1. Agree a lot	271	29.6
2. Agree a little	250	27.4
3. Disagree a little	183	20.0
4. Disagree a lot	202	22.1
TOTAL	914	100.0

Mean	2.328	Std. err.	0.038
Mode	1.000	Std. dev.	1.144
Kurtosis	-1.278	Skewness	0.186
Median	2.212	Variance	1.309

Range for computation of statistics: 1 through 4.

TABLE III-8(t): GROUP III (Spring, 1973).

Category Label	n	%
0. No response	18	1.8
1. Agree a lot	239	24.3
2. Agree a little	295	30.0
3. Disagree a little	216	22.0
4. Disagree a lot	216	22.0
TOTAL	984	100.0

Mean	2.379	Std. err.	0.036
Mode	2.000	Std. dev.	1.127
Kurtosis	-1.130	Skewness	0.061
Median	2.297	Variance	1.271

Range for computation of statistics: 1 through 4.

Q. 8(u). Right to strike: general laborers.[70]

TABLE II-8(u): GROUP II (Fall, 1972).

Category Label	n	%
0. No response	8	0.9
1. Agree a lot	501	54.8
2. Agree a little	325	35.6
3. Disagree a little	62	6.8
4. Disagree a lot	18	2.0
TOTAL	914	100.0

Mean	1.542	Std. err.	0.024
Mode	1.000	Std. dev.	0.721
Kurtosis	1.212	Skewness	1.116
Median	1.396	Variance	0.520

Range for computation of statistics: 1 through 4.

TABLE III-8(u): GROUP III (Spring, 1973).

Category Label	n	%
0. No response	16	1.6
1. Agree a lot	547	55.6
2. Agree a little	342	34.8
3. Disagree a little	61	6.2
4. Disagree a lot	18	1.8
TOTAL	984	100.0

Mean	1.510	Std. err.	0.023
Mode	1.000	Std. dev.	0.719
Kurtosis	1.315	Skewness	1.074
Median	1.370	Variance	0.517

Range for computation of statistics: 1 through 4.

Q. 8(v). If majority vote, should be required to join.[71]

TABLE II-8(v): GROUP II (Fall, 1972).

Category Label	n	%
0. No response	10	1.1
1. Agree a lot	233	25.5
2. Agree a little	265	29.0
3. Disagree a little	197	21.6
4. Disagree a lot	209	22.9
TOTAL	914	100.0

Mean	2.396	Std. err.	0.037
Mode	2.000	Std. dev.	1.128
Kurtosis	-1.223	Skewness	0.090
Median	2.308	Variance	1.273

Range for computation of statistics: 1 through 4.

TABLE III-8(v): GROUP III (Spring, 1973).

Category Label	n	5
0. No response	20	2.0
1. Agree a lot	300	30.5
2. Agree a little	294	29.9
3. Disagree a little	199	20.2
4. Disagree a lot	171	17.4
TOTAL	984	100.0

Mean	2.204	Std. err.	0.036
Mode	1.000	Std. dev.	1.115
Kurtosis	-1.050	Skewness	0.257
Median	2.085	Variance	1.243

Range for computation of statistics: 1 through 4.

Q. 8(w). Right to strike: military personnel. [72]

TABLE II-8(w): GROUP II (Fall, 1972).

Category Label	n	%
0. No response	14	1.5
1. Agree a lot	200	21.9
2. Agree a little	201	22.0
3. Disagree a little	238	26.0
4. Disagree a lot	261	28.6
TOTAL	914	100.0

Mean	2.582	Std. err.	0.038
Mode	4.000	Std. dev.	1.160
Kurtosis	-1.209	Skewness	-0.218
Median	2.676	Variance	1.345

Range for computation of statistics: 1 through 4.

TABLE III-8(w): GROUP III (Spring, 1973).

Category Label	n	%
0. No response	30	3.0
1. Agree a lot	213	21.6
2. Agree a little	228	23.2
3. Disagree a little	236	24.0
4. Disagree a lot	277	28.2
TOTAL	984	100.0

Mean	2.525	Std. err.	0.038
Mode	4.000	Std. dev.	1.196
Kurtosis	-1.152	Skewness	-0.214
Median	2.589	Variance	1.430

Range for computation of statistics: 1 through 4.

Q. 8(x). Right to strike: post office workers. [73]

TABLE II-8(x): GROUP II (Fall, 1972).

Category Label	n	%
0. No response	19	2.1
1. Agree a lot	289	31.6
2. Agree a little	293	32.1
3. Disagree a little	172	18.8
4. Disagree a lot	141	15.4
TOTAL	914	100.0

Mean	2.139	Std. err.	0.036
Mode	2.000	Std. dev.	1.089
Kurtosis	-0.923	Skewness	0.343
Median	2.009	Variance	1.187

Range for computation of statistics: 1 through 4.

TABLE III-8(x): GROUP III (Spring, 1972).

Category Label	n	%
0. No response	25	2.5
1. Agree a lot	324	32.9
2. Agree a little	353	35.9
3. Disagree a little	174	17.7
4. Disagree a lot	108	11.0
TOTAL	984	100.0

Mean	2.016	Std. err.	0.033
Mode	2.000	Std. dev.	1.023
Kurtosis	-0.595	Skewness	0.440
Median	1.905	Variance	1.048

Range for computation of statistics: 1 through 4.

Q. 8(y).   Unions do more harm than good.[74]

TABLE II-8(y):   GROUP II (Fall, 1972).

Category Label		n	%
0.	No response	32	3.5
1.	Agree a lot	63	6.9
2.	Agree a little	234	25.6
3.	Disagree a little	444	48.6
4.	Disagree a lot	141	15.4
TOTAL		914	100.0
Mean	2.655	Std. err.	0.031
Mode	3.000	Std. dev.	0.940
Kurtosis	0.614	Skewness	-0.778
Median	2.788	Variance	0.883

Range for computation of statistics: 1 through 4.

TABLE III-8(y):   GROUP III (Spring, 1973).

Category Label		n	%
0.	No response	44	4.5
1.	Agree a lot	51	5.2
2.	Agree a little	221	22.5
3.	Disagree a little	482	49.0
4.	Disagree a lot	186	18.9
TOTAL		984	100.0
Mean	2.727	Std. err.	0.031
Mode	3.000	Std. dev.	0.974
Kurtosis	0.879	Skewness	-0.929
Median	2.865	Variance	0.950

Range for computation of statistics: 1 through 4.

Q. 8(z). Labor trouble is due to radical agitators.[75]

TABLE II-8(z): GROUP II (Fall, 1972).

Category Label	n	%
0. No response	22	2.4
1. Agree a lot	109	11.9
2. Agree a little	284	31.1
3. Disagree a little	310	33.9
4. Disagree a lot	189	20.7
TOTAL	914	100.0

Mean	2.585	Std. err.	0.034
Mode	3.000	Std. dev.	1.020
Kurtosis	-0.500	Skewness	-0.324
Median	2.635	Variance	1.040

Range for computation of statistics: 1 through 4.

TABLE III-8(z): GROUP III (Spring, 1973).

Category Label	n	%
0. No response	44	4.5
1. Agree a lot	115	11.7
2. Agree a little	262	26.6
3. Disagree a little	318	32.3
4. Disagree a lot	245	24.9
TOTAL	984	100.0

Mean	2.615	Std. err.	0.035
Mode	3.000	Std. dev.	1.113
Kurtosis	-0.488	Skewness	-0.489
Median	2.723	Variance	1.238

Range for computation of statistics: 1 through 4.

LABOR POLICY

Q. 8(aa). Go too far when can't fire workers.[76]

TABLE II-8(aa): GROUP II (Fall, 1972).

Category Label	n	%
0. No response	18	2.0
1. Agree a lot	120	13.1
2. Agree a little	289	31.6
3. Disagree a little	312	34.1
4. Disagree a lot	175	19.1
TOTAL	914	100.0

Mean	2.554	Std. err.	0.033
Mode	3.000	Std. dev.	1.006
Kurtosis	-0.572	Skewness	-0.260
Median	2.596	Variance	1.012

Range for computation of statistics: 1 through 4.

TABLE III-8(aa): GROUP III (Spring, 1973).

Category Label	n	%
0. No response	34	3.5
1. Agree a lot	120	12.2
2. Agree a little	289	29.4
3. Disagree a little	340	34.6
4. Disagree a lot	201	20.4
TOTAL	984	100.0

Mean	2.563	Std. err.	0.034
Mode	3.000	Std. dev.	1.052
Kurtosis	-0.441	Skewness	-0.400
Median	2.644	Variance	1.107

Range for computation of statistics: 1 through 4.

Q. 8(bb). Right to strike: garbage workers. 77

TABLE II-8(bb): GROUP II (Fall, 1972).

Category Label	n	%
0. No response	14	1.5
1. Agree a lot	497	54.4
2. Agree a little	264	28.9
3. Disagree a little	87	9.5
4. Disagree a lot	52	5.7
TOTAL	914	100.0

Mean	1.635	Std. err.	0.029
Mode	1.000	Std. dev.	0.892
Kurtosis	0.665	Skewness	1.135
Median	1.391	Variance	0.795

Range for computation of statistics: 1 through 4.

TABLE III-8(bb): GROUP III (Spring, 1973).

Category Label	n	%
0. No response	28	2.8
1. Agree a lot	493	50.1
2. Agree a little	332	33.7
3. Disagree a little	75	7.6
4. Disagree a lot	56	5.7
TOTAL	984	100.0

Mean	1.632	Std. err.	0.028
Mode	1.000	Std. dev.	0.886
Kurtosis	0.816	Skewness	1.034
Median	1.441	Variance	0.784

Range for computation of statistics: 1 through 4.

Q. 8(cc). Must crush general strike at all costs. [78]

TABLE II-8(cc): GROUP II (Fall, 1972).

Category Label	n	%
0. No response	27	3.0
1. Agree a lot	98	10.7
2. Agree a little	206	22.5
3. Disagree a little	302	33.0
4. Disagree a lot	281	30.7
TOTAL	914	100.0

Mean	2.779	Std. err.	0.036
Mode	3.000	Std. dev.	1.086
Kurtosis	-0.410	Skewness	-0.610
Median	2.917	Variance	1.180

Range for computation of statistics: 1 through 4.

TABLE III-8(cc): GROUP III (Spring, 1973).

Category Label	n	%
0. No response	36	3.7
1. Agree a lot	86	8.7
2. Agree a little	159	16.2
3. Disagree a little	357	36.3
4. Disagree a lot	346	35.2
TOTAL	984	100.0

Mean	2.905	Std. err.	0.035
Mode	3.000	Std. dev.	1.088
Kurtosis	0.121	Skewness	-0.901
Median	3.091	Variance	1.184

Range for computation of statistics: 1 through 4.

PREFERENCES FOR
THE PRESIDENCY

Q. 9.   Democratic nominee preference.[79]

TABLE II-9:   GROUP II (Fall, 1972).

Category Label	n	%
0. No response	75	8.2
1. Chisholm	276	30.2
2. Hartke	0	0.0
3. Humphrey	59	6.5
4. Jackson	4	0.4
5. Kennedy	389	42.6
6. Lindsay	14	1.5
7. McCarthy	3	0.3
8. McGovern	72	7.9
9. Maddox	0	0.0
10. Mills	0	0.0
11. Muskie	18	2.0
12. Sanford	1	0.1
13. Wallace	3	0.3
14. Yorty	0	0.0
TOTAL	914	100.0

Q. 9. Democratic nominee preference. [79]

TABLE III-9: GROUP III (Spring, 1973).

Category Label	n	%
0. No response	87	8.8
1. Chisholm	257	26.1
2. Hartke	1	0.1
3. Humphrey	94	9.6
4. Jackson	2	0.2
5. Kennedy	417	42.4
6. Lindsay	9	0.9
7. McCarthy	4	0.4
8. McGovern	92	9.3
9. Maddox	0	0.0
10. Mills	1	0.1
11. Muskie	13	1.3
12. Sanford	3	0.3
13. Wallace	4	0.4
14. Yorty	0	0.0
TOTAL	984	100.0

Q. 10(a).   2-way race 1972, Chisholm-Nixon.[80]

TABLE II-10(a):   GROUP II (Fall, 1972).

Category Label	n	%
0. No response	277	30.3
1. Chisholm	554	60.6
2. Nixon	83	9.1
TOTAL	914	100.0

TABLE III-10(a):   GROUP III (Spring, 1973).

Category Label	n	%
0. No response	218	22.2
1. Chisholm	700	71.1
2. Nixon	66	6.7
TOTAL	984	100.0

PREFERENCES IN TWO-WAY RACES IN 1972
Q. 10(b).   2-way race 1972, Hartke-Nixon.[80]

TABLE II-10(b):   GROUP II (Fall, 1972).

Category Label	n	%
0. No response	430	47.0
1. Hartke	199	21.8
2. Nixon	285	31.2
TOTAL	914	100.0

TABLE III-10(b):   GROUP III (Spring, 1973).

Category Label	n	%
0. No response	355	36.1
1. Hartke	379	38.5
2. Nixon	250	25.4
TOTAL	984	100.0

PREFERENCES IN TWO-WAY RACES IN 1972 269

Q. 10(c). 2-way race 1972, Humphrey-Nixon.[80]

TABLE II-10(c): GROUP II (Fall, 1972).

Category Label	n	%
0. No response	360	39.4
1. Humphrey	496	54.3
2. Nixon	58	6.3
TOTAL	914	100.0

TABLE III-10(c): GROUP III (Spring, 1973).

Category Label	n	%
0. No response	247	25.1
1. Humphrey	697	70.8
2. Nixon	40	4.1
TOTAL	984	100.0

PREFERENCES IN TWO-WAY RACES IN 1972

Q. 10(d). 2-way race 1972, Jackson-Nixon.[80]

TABLE II-10(d): GROUP II (Fall, 1972).

Category Label	n	%
0. No response	416	45.5
1. Jackson	272	29.8
2. Nixon	226	24.7
TOTAL	914	100.0

TABLE III-10(d): GROUP III (Spring, 1973).

Category Label	n	%
0. No response	353	35.9
1. Jackson	439	44.6
2. Nixon	192	19.5
TOTAL	984	100.0

Q. 10(e).   2-way race 1972, Kennedy-Nixon. [80]

TABLE II-10(e):   GROUP II (Fall, 1972).

Category Label	n	%
0. No response	235	25.7
1. Kennedy	664	72.6
2. Nixon	15	1.6
TOTAL	914	100.0

TABLE III-10(e):   GROUP III (Spring, 1973).

Category Label	n	%
0. No response	159	16.2
1. Kennedy	812	82.5
2. Nixon	13	1.3
TOTAL	984	100.0

PREFERENCES IN TWO-WAY RACES IN 1972
Q. 10(f).   2-way race 1972, Lindsay-Nixon. [80]

TABLE II-10(f):   GROUP II (Fall, 1972).

Category Label	n	%
0. No response	403	44.1
1. Lindsay	369	40.4
2. Nixon	142	15.5
TOTAL	914	100.0

TABLE III-10(f):   GROUP III (Spring, 1973).

Category Label	n	%
0. No response	314	31.9
1. Lindsay	555	56.4
2. Nixon	115	11.7
TOTAL	984	100.0

Q. 10(g). 2-way race 1972, McCarthy-Nixon. [80]

TABLE II-10(g): GROUP II (Fall, 1972).

Category Label	n	%
0. No response	399	43.7
1. McCarthy	385	42.1
2. Nixon	130	14.2
TOTAL	914	100.0

TABLE III-10(g): GROUP III (Spring, 1973).

Category Label	n	%
0. No response	300	30.5
1. McCarthy	574	58.3
2. Nixon	110	11.2
TOTAL	984	100.0

PREFERENCES IN TWO-WAY RACES IN 1972
Q. 10(h). 2-way race 1972, McGovern-Nixon.[80]

TABLE II-10(h): GROUP II (FALL, 1972).

Category Label	n	%
0. No response	331	36.2
1. McGovern	506	55.4
2. Nixon	77	8.4
TOTAL	914	100.0

TABLE III-10(h): GROUP III (Spring, 1973).

Category Label	n	%
0. No response	262	26.6
1. McGovern	667	67.8
2. Nixon	55	5.6
TOTAL	984	100.0

Q. 10(i).   2-way race 1972, Maddox-Nixon.[80]

TABLE II-10(i): GROUP II (Fall, 1972).

Category Label	n	%
0. No response	415	45.4
1. Maddox	135	14.8
2. Nixon	364	39.8
TOTAL	914	100.0

TABLE III-10(i): GROUP III (Spring, 1973).

Category Label	n	%
0. No response	332	33.7
1. Maddox	230	23.4
2. Nixon	422	42.9
TOTAL	984	100.0

PREFERENCES IN TWO-WAY RACES IN 1972
Q. 10(j).   2-way race 1972, Mills-Nixon.[80]

TABLE II-10(j): GROUP II (Fall, 1972).

Category Label	n	%
0. No response	431	47.2
1. Mills	222	24.3
2. Nixon	261	28.6
TOTAL	914	100.0

TABLE III-10(j): GROUP III (Spring, 1973).

Category Label	n	%
0. No response	364	37.0
1. Mills	392	39.8
2. Nixon	228	23.2
TOTAL	984	100.0

Q. 10(k).   2-way race 1972, Muskie-Nixon. 80

TABLE II-10(k):   GROUP II (Fall, 1972).

Category Label	n	%
0. No response	397	43.4
1. Muskie	399	43.7
2. Nixon	118	12.9
TOTAL	914	100.0

TABLE III-10(k):   GROUP III (Spring, 1973).

Category Label	n	%
0. No response	304	30.9
1. Muskie	592	60.2
2. Nixon	88	8.9
TOTAL	984	100.0

PREFERENCES IN TWO-WAY RACES IN 1972
Q. 10(1).   2-way race 1972, Sanford-Nixon. 80

TABLE II-10(1):   GROUP II (Fall, 1972).

Category Label	n	%
0. No response	436	47.7
1. Sanford	207	22.6
2. Nixon	271	29.6
TOTAL	914	100.0

TABLE III-10(1):   GROUP III (Spring, 1973).

Category Label	n	%
0. No response	355	36.1
1. Sanford	415	42.2
2. Nixon	214	21.7
TOTAL	984	100.0

Q. 10(m).   2-way race 1972, Wallace-Nixon. [80]

TABLE II-10(m):   GROUP II (Fall, 1972).

Category Label	n	%
0. No response	417	45.6
1. Wallace	49	5.4
2. Nixon	448	49.0
TOTAL	914	100.0

TABLE III-10(m):   GROUP III (Spring, 1973).

Category Label	n	%
0. No response	330	33.5
1. Wallace	138	14.0
2. Nixon	516	52.4
TOTAL	984	100.0

PREFERENCES IN TWO-WAY RACES IN 1972
Q. 10(n).   2-way race 1972, Yorty-Nixon. [80]

TABLE II-10(n):   GROUP II (Fall, 1972).

Category Label	n	%
0. No response	421	46.1
1. Yorty	212	23.2
2. Nixon	281	30.7
TOTAL	914	100.0

TABLE III-10(n):   GROUP III (Spring, 1973).

Category Label	n	%
0. No response	353	35.9
1. Yorty	364	37.0
2. Nixon	267	27.1
TOTAL	984	100.0

Q. 11(a). 3-way race 1972, Chisholm-Nixon-Wallace.[81]

TABLE II-11(a): GROUP II (Fall, 1972).

Category Label	n	%
0. No response	274	30.0
1. Chisholm	558	61.1
2. Nixon	78	8.5
3. Wallace	4	0.4
TOTAL	914	100.0

TABLE III-11(a): GROUP III (Spring, 1973).

Category Label	n	%
0. No response	231	23.5
1. Chisholm	682	69.3
2. Nixon	63	6.4
3. Wallace	8	0.8
TOTAL	984	100.0

Q. 11(b).   3-way race 1972, Hartke-Nixon-Wallace. [81]

TABLE II-11(b):   GROUP II (Fall, 1972)

Category Label	n	%
0. No response	405	44.3
1. Hartke	208	22.8
2. Nixon	290	31.7
3. Wallace	11	1.2
TOTAL	914	100.0

TABLE III-11(b):   GROUP III (Spring, 1973).

Category Label	n	%
0. No response	346	35.2
1. Hartke	378	38.4
2. Nixon	237	24.1
3. Wallace	23	2.3
TOTAL	984	100.0

Q. 11(c).   3-way race 1972, Humphrey-Nixon-Wallace. [81]

TABLE II-11(c):   GROUP II (Fall, 1972).

Category Label	n	%
0. No response	341	37.3
1. Humphrey	519	56.8
2. Nixon	51	5.6
3. Wallace	3	0.3
TOTAL	914	100.0

TABLE III-11(c):   GROUP III (Spring, 1973).

Category Label	n	%
0. No response	238	24.2
1. Humphrey	703	71.4
2. Nixon	36	3.7
3. Wallace	7	0.7
TOTAL	984	100.0

Q. 11(d).   3-way race 1972, Jackson–Nixon–Wallace. [81]

TABLE II-11(d):   GROUP II (Fall, 1972).

Category Label	n	%
0. No response	407	44.5
1. Jackson	285	31.2
2. Nixon	214	23.4
3. Wallace	8	0.9
TOTAL	914	100.0

TABLE III-11(d):   GROUP III (Spring, 1973).

Category Label	n	%
0. No response	339	34.5
1. Jackson	454	46.1
2. Nixon	175	17.8
3. Wallace	16	1.6
TOTAL	984	100.0

Q. 11(e).   3-way race 1972, Kennedy-Nixon-Wallace. [81]

TABLE II-11(e):   GROUP II (Fall, 1972).

Category Label	n	%
0. No response	227	24.8
1. Kennedy	673	73.6
2. Nixon	12	1.3
3. Wallace	2	0.2
TOTAL	914	100.0

TABLE III-11(e):   GROUP III (Spring, 1973).

Category Label	n	%
0. No response	153	15.5
1. Kennedy	821	83.4
2. Nixon	9	0.9
3. Wallace	1	0.1
TOTAL	984	100.0

Q. 11(f).   3-way race 1972, Lindsay-Nixon-Wallace. [81]

TABLE II-11(f): GROUP II (Fall, 1972).

Category Label	n	%
0. No response	382	41.8
1. Lindsay	389	42.6
2. Nixon	136	14.9
3. Wallace	7	0.8
TOTAL	914	100.0

TABLE III-11(f): GROUP III (Spring, 1973).

Category Label	n	%
0. No response	305	31.0
1. Lindsay	558	56.7
2. Nixon	113	11.5
3. Wallace	8	0.8
TOTAL	984	100.0

Q. 11(g).   3-way race 1972, McCarthy-Nixon-Wallace. [81]

TABLE II-11(g):   GROUP II (Fall, 1972).

Category Label	n	%
0. No response	386	42.2
1. McCarthy	399	43.7
2. Nixon	124	13.6
3. Wallace	5	0.5
TOTAL	914	100.0

TABLE III-11(g):   GROUP III (Spring, 1973).

Category Label	n	%
0. No response	294	29.9
1 McCarthy	593	60.3
2. Nixon	89	9.0
3. Wallace	8	0.8
TOTAL	984	100.0

Q. 11(h). 3-way race 1972, McGovern-Nixon-Wallace. [81]

TABLE II-11(h): GROUP II (Fall, 1972).

Category Label	n	%
0. No response	312	34.1
1. McGovern	528	57.8
2. Nixon	68	7.4
3. Wallace	6	0.7
TOTAL	914	100.0

TABLE III-11(h): GROUP III (Spring, 1973).

Category Label	n	%
0. No response	251	25.5
1. McGovern	682	69.3
2. Nixon	47	4.8
3. Wallace	4	0.4
TOTAL	984	100.0

Q. 11(i).   3-way race 1972, Maddox-Nixon-Wallace. [81]

TABLE II-11(i):   GROUP II (Fall, 1972).

Category Label	n	%
0. No response	403	44.1
1. Maddox	141	15.4
2. Nixon	358	39.2
3. Wallace	12	1.3
TOTAL	914	100.0

TABLE III-11(i):   GROUP III (Spring, 1973).

Category Label	n	%
0. No response	341	34.7
1. Maddox	229	23.3
2. Nixon	383	38.9
3. Wallace	31	3.2
TOTAL	984	100.0

Q. 11(j). 3-way race 1972, Mills-Nixon-Wallace.[81]

TABLE II-11(j): GROUP II (Fall, 1972).

Category Label	n	%
0. No response	406	44.4
1. Mills	231	25.3
2. Nixon	268	29.3
3. Wallace	9	1.0
TOTAL	914	100.0

TABLE III-11(j): GROUP III (Spring, 1973).

Category Label	n	%
0. No response	348	35.4
1. Mills	387	39.3
2. Nixon	232	23.6
3. Wallace	17	1.7
TOTAL	984	100.0

Q. 11(k). 3-way race 1972, Muskie-Nixon-Wallace. [81]

TABLE II-11(k): GROUP II (Fall, 1972).

Category Label	n	%
0. No response	379	41.5
1. Muskie	421	46.1
2. Nixon	111	12.1
3. Wallace	3	0.3
TOTAL	914	100.0

TABLE II-11(k): GROUP III (Spring, 1973).

Category Label	n	%
0. No response	297	30.2
1. Muskie	591	60.1
2. Nixon	89	9.0
3. Wallace	7	0.7
TOTAL	984	100.0

Q. 11(1).   3-way race 1972, Sanford-Nixon-Wallace. [81]

TABLE II-11(1):   GROUP II (Fall, 1972).

Category Label	n	%
0. No response	406	44.4
1. Sanford	218	23.9
2. Nixon	282	30.9
3. Wallace	8	0.9
TOTAL	914	100.0

TABLE III-11(1):   GROUP III (Spring, 1973).

Category Label	n	%
0. No response	341	34.7
1. Sanford	412	41.9
2. Nixon	210	21.3
3. Wallace	21	2.1
TOTAL	984	100.0

Q. 11(m).   3-way race 1972, Yorty-Nixon-Wallace.[81]

TABLE II-11(m): GROUP II (Fall, 1972).

Category Label	n	%
0. No response	403	44.1
1. Yorty	215	23.5
2. Nixon	285	31.2
3. Wallace	11	1.2
TOTAL	914	100.0

TABLE III-11(m): GROUP III (Spring, 1973).

Category Label	n	%
0. No response	343	34.9
1. Yorty	365	37.1
2. Nixon	255	25.9
3. Wallace	21	2.1
TOTAL	914	100.0

SOCIODEMOGRAPHIC CHARACTERISTICS

Q. 12.   Age of respondent.[82]

TABLE II-12:   GROUP II (Fall, 1972).

Category Label	n	%
0. No response	22	2.4
1. 18–25	848	92.8
2. 26–29	23	2.5
3. 30–34	11	1.2
4. 35–39	5	0.5
5. 40–44	1	0.1
6. 45–49	0	0.0
7. 50–59	4	0.4
TOTAL	914	100.0

Mean	1.072	Std. err.	0.019
Mode	1.000	Std. dev.	0.563
Kurtosis	59.671	Skewness	6.689
Median	1.013	Variance	0.317

Range for computation of statistics: 1 through 7.

TABLE III-12:   GROUP III (Spring, 1973).

Category Label	n	%
0. No response	17	1.7
1. 18–25	860	87.4
2. 26–29	67	6.8
3. 30–34	28	2.8
4. 35–39	5	0.5
5. 40–44	2	0.2
6. 45–49	4	0.4
7. 50–59	1	0.1
TOTAL	984	100.0

Mean	1.158	Std. err.	0.020
Mode	1.000	Std. dev.	0.625
Kurtosis	27.005	Skewness	4.437
Median	1.052	Variance	0.391

Range for computation of statistics: 1 through 7.

Q. 13. Marital status of respondent.[83]

TABLE II-13: GROUP II (Fall, 1972).

Category Label	n	%
0. No response	7	0.8
1. Married	107	11.7
2. Divorced	8	0.9
3. Single	780	85.3
4. Widowed	0	0.0
5. Separated	5	0.5
6. Common law	7	0.8
TOTAL	914	100.0

TABLE III-13: GROUP III (Spring, 1973).

Category Label	n	%
0. No response	6	0.6
1. Married	145	14.7
2. Divorced	19	1.9
3. Single	788	80.1
4. Widowed	7	0.7
5. Separated	13	1.3
6. Common law	6	0.6
TOTAL	984	100.0

Q. 14(a). Region of respondent's residence.

TABLE II-14(a): GROUP II (Fall, 1972).

Category Label	n	%
0. No response	6	0.7
1. Northeast	9	1.0
2. Midwest	34	3.7
3. Great Plains	2	0.2
4. South	682	74.6
5. Border	175	19.1
6. Rocky Mountain	0	0.0
7. Pacific Coast	4	0.4
8. Non-contiguous	0	0.0
9. Foreign	2	0.2
TOTAL	914	100.0

TABLE III-14(a): GROUP III (Spring, 1973).

Category Label	n	%
0. No response	14	1.4
1. Northeast	20	2.0
2. Midwest	14	1.4
3. Great Plains	1	0.1
4. South	909	92.4
5. Border	11	1.1
6. Rocky Mountain	1	0.1
7. Pacific Coast	11	1.1
8. Non-contiguous	2	0.2
9. Foreign	1	0.1
TOTAL	984	100.0

Q. 14(b). State of respondent's residence.[84]

TABLE II-14(b): GROUP II (Fall, 1972).

Category Label	n	%
0. No response	4	0.4
1. Connecticut	1	0.1
3. Massachusetts	1	0.1
12. New Jersey	2	0.2
13. New York	5	0.5
14. Pennsylvania	2	0.2
21. Illinois	17	1.9
22. Indiana	3	0.3
23. Michigan	7	0.8
24. Ohio	7	0.8
34. Missouri	2	0.2
40. Virginia	3	0.3
41. Alabama	195	21.3
42. Arkansas	2	0.2
43. Florida	79	8.6
44. Georgia	12	1.3
45. Louisiana	205	22.4
46. Mississippi	158	17.3
48. South Carolina	22	2.4
49. Texas	6	0.7
51. Kentucky	3	0.3
53. Oklahoma	2	0.2
54. Tennessee	168	18.4
55. District of Columbia	2	0.2
71. California	4	0.4
99. Foreign	2	0.2
TOTAL	914	100.0

Q. 14(b). State of respondent's residence.[84]

TABLE III-14(b): GROUP III (Spring, 1973).

Category Label	n	%
0. No response	8	0.8
1. Connecticut	4	0.4
3. Massachusetts	2	0.2
11. Delaware	1	0.1
12. New Jersey	5	0.5
13. New York	7	0.7
14. Pennsylvania	7	0.7
21. Illinois	6	0.6
22. Indiana	3	0.3
23. Michigan	1	0.1
24. Ohio	4	0.4
34. Missouri	1	0.1
40. Virginia	137	13.9
41. Alabama	7	0.7
42. Arkansas	96	9.8
43. Florida	17	1.7
44. Georgia	24	2.4
45. Louisiana	11	1.1
46. Mississippi	9	0.9
47. North Carolina	142	14.4
48. South Carolina	196	19.9
49. Texas	270	27.4
51. Kentucky	1	0.1
52. Maryland	2	0.2
53. Oklahoma	2	0.2
54. Tennessee	2	0.2
55. District of Columbia	4	0.4
62. Colorado	1	0.1
71. California	11	1.1
82. Hawaii	2	0.2
99. Foreign	1	0.1
TOTAL	984	100.0

Q. 15.   Population of R's home community. [85]

TABLE II-15:   GROUP II (Fall, 1972).

Category Label	n	%
0. No response	29	3.2
1. 1-2,499	138	15.1
2. 2,500-9,999	202	22.1
3. 10,000-24,999	172	18.8
4. 25,000-99,999	108	11.8
5. 100,000-249,999	75	8.2
6. 250,000-499,999	71	7.8
7. 500,000-Million	80	8.8
8. Over a million	39	4.3
TOTAL	914	100.0

Mean	3.461	Std. err.	0.070
Mode	2.000	Std. dev.	2.125
Kurtosis	-0.710	Skewness	0.541
Median	3.012	Variance	4.516

Range for computation of statistics: 1 through 8.

TABLE III-15:   GROUP III (Spring, 1973).

Category Label	n	%
0. No response	43	4.4
1. 1-2,499	129	13.1
2. 2,500-9,999	219	22.3
3. 10,000-24,999	138	14.0
4. 25,000-99,999	124	12.6
5. 100,000-249,999	90	9.1
6. 250,000-499,999	60	6.1
7. 500,000-Million	59	6.0
8. Over a million	122	12.4
TOTAL	984	100.0

Mean	3.736	Std. err.	0.076
Mode	2.000	Std. dev.	2.388
Kurtosis	-0.922	Skewness	0.471
Median	3.232	Variance	5.704

Range for computation of statistics: 1 through 8.

Q. 16.   Level of education R wants to complete.[86]

TABLE II-16:   GROUP II (Fall, 1972).

Category Label	n	%
0. No response	35	3.8
1. No degree	28	3.1
2. Bachelors	118	12.9
3. Masters	391	42.8
4. Prof. or PhD.	342	37.4
TOTAL	914	100.0

Mean	3.191	Std. err.	0.026
Mode	3.000	Std. dev.	0.784
Kurtosis	0.102	Skewness	-0.746
Median	3.251	Variance	0.615

Range for computation of statistics: 1 through 4.

TABLE III-16:   GROUP III (Spring, 1973).

Category Label	n	%
0. No response	28	2.8
1. No degree	24	2.4
2. Bachelors	132	13.4
3. Masters	392	39.8
4. Prof. or PhD.	408	41.5
TOTAL	984	100.0

Mean	3.238	Std. err.	0.025
Mode	4.000	Std. dev.	0.780
Kurtosis	-0.031	Skewness	-0.760
Median	3.321	Variance	0.609

Range for computation of statistics: 1 through 4.

Q. 17.   Year of college in which enrolled.[87]

TABLE II-17:   GROUP II (Fall, 1972).

Category Label	n	%
0. No response	2	0.2
1. Freshman	210	23.0
2. Sophomore	324	35.4
3. Junior	221	24.2
4. Senior	151	16.5
5. Masters	6	0.7
TOTAL	914	100.0

Mean	2.358	Std. err.	0.034
Mode	2.000	Std. dev.	1.036
Kurtosis	-0.900	Skewness	0.267
Median	2.256	Variance	1.073

Range for computation of statistics: 1 through 5.

TABLE III-17:   GROUP III (Spring, 1973).

Category Label	n	%
0. No response	6	0.6
1. Freshman	230	23.4
2. Sophomore	321	32.6
3. Junior	267	27.1
4. Senior	149	15.1
5. Masters	11	1.1
TOTAL	984	100.0

Mean	2.362	Std. err.	0.034
Mode	2.000	Std. dev.	1.052
Kurtosis	-0.810	Skewness	0.220
Median	2.298	Variance	1.106

Range for computation of statistics: 1 through 5.

Q. 18.   Level of father's education.[88]

TABLE II-18:   GROUP II (Fall, 1972).

Category Label	n	%
0. No response	4	0.4
1. None	19	2.1
2. Grade school only	225	24.6
3. Some high school	274	30.0
4. High school	180	19.7
5. HS + non-college	44	4.8
6. College, no degree	77	8.4
7. Bachelors	40	4.4
8. Bachelor + Masters	35	3.8
9. Bach. + PhD, Prof.	16	1.8
TOTAL	914	100.0

Mean	3.717	Std. err.	0.060
Mode	3.000	Std. dev.	1.815
Kurtosis	0.526	Skewness	1.047
Median	3.263	Variance	3.294

Range for computation of statistics: 1 through 9.

TABLE III-18:   GROUP III (Spring, 1973).

Category Label	n	%
0. No response	14	1.4
1. None	35	3.6
2. Grade school only	245	24.9
3. Some high school	229	23.3
4. High school	174	17.7
5. HS + non-college	66	6.7
6. College, no degree	114	11.6
7. Bachelors	52	5.3
8. Bachelor + Masters	44	4.5
9. Bach. + Phd, Prof.	11	1.1
TOTAL	984	100.0

Mean	3.798	Std. err.	0.062
Mode	2.000	Std. dev.	1.934
Kurtosis	-0.253	Skewness	0.672
Median	3.365	Variance	3.740

Range for computation of statistics: 1 through 9.

Q. 19. Level of mother's education.[89]

TABLE II-19: GROUP II (Fall, 1972).

Category Label	n	%
0. No response	8	0.9
1. None	3	0.3
2. Grade school only	127	13.9
3. Some high school	287	31.4
4. High school	210	23.0
5. HS + non-college	69	7.5
6. College, no degree	101	11.1
7. Bachelors	62	6.8
8. Bachelor + Masters	33	3.6
9. Bach. + PhD, Prof.	14	1.5
TOTAL	914	100.0

Mean	4.084	Std. err.	0.058
Mode	3.000	Std. dev.	1.768
Kurtosis	0.042	Skewness	0.753
Median	3.652	Variance	3.124

Range for computation of statistics: 1 through 9.

TABLE III-19: GROUP III (Spring, 1973).

Category Label	n	%
0. No response	13	1.3
1. None	8	0.8
2. Grade school only	100	10.2
3. Some high school	269	27.3
4. High school	257	26.1
5. HS + non-college	97	9.9
6. College, no degree	107	10.9
7. Bachelors	67	6.8
8. Bachelor + Masters	57	5.8
9. Bach. + PhD, Prof.	9	0.9
TOTAL	984	100.0

Mean	4.244	Std. err.	0.057
Mode	3.000	Std. dev.	1.792
Kurtosis	-0.122	Skewness	0.547
Median	3.897	Variance	3.210

Range for computation of statistics: 1 through 9.

Q. 20.   Field of study in which enrolled.[90]

TABLE II-20:   GROUP II   (Fall, 1972).

Category Label	n	%
0. No response	14	1.5
1. Agriculture	34	3.7
2. Arts and Sciences	358	39.2
3. Business Admin.	128	14.0
4. Education	260	28.4
5. Engineering	19	2.1
6. Graduate	6	0.7
7. Home Economics	21	2.3
8. Nursing	11	1.2
9. Other	63	6.9
TOTAL	914	100.0

TABLE III-20:   GROUP III (Spring, 1973).

Category Label	n	%
0. No response	22	2.2
1. Agriculture	14	1.4
2. Arts and Sciences	474	48.2
3. Business Admin.	138	14.0
4. Education	206	20.9
5. Engineering	25	2.5
6. Graduate	10	1.0
7. Home Economics	28	2.8
8. Nursing	15	1.5
9. Other	52	5.3
TOTAL	984	100.0

Q. 21. Expected occupational field.[91]

TABLE II-21: GROUP II (Fall, 1972).

Category Label	n	%
0. No response	27	3.0
1. Prof., Technical	574	62.8
2. Mgr., Official, Prop.	105	11.5
3. Clerical, Sales	53	5.8
4. Crafts, Fore., Mech.	10	1.1
5. Mach. Opr., Driver	6	0.7
6. HH Serv., Mil., Police	34	3.7
7. Laborer, Teamster	2	0.2
8. Farm Mgr., Worker	5	0.5
9. Not in work force	98	10.7
TOTAL	914	100.0

TABLE III-21: GROUP III (Spring, 1973).

Category Label	n	%
0. No response	19	1.9
1. Prof. Technical	727	73.9
2. Mgr., Official, Prop.	83	8.4
3. Clerical, Sales	56	5.7
4. Crafts, Fore., Mech.	10	1.0
5. Mach. Opr., Driver	2	0.2
6. HH Serv., Mil., Police	28	2.8
7. Laborer, Teamster	2	0.2
8. Farm Mgr., Worker	1	0.1
9. Not in work force	56	5.7
TOTAL	984	100.0

Q. 22. Occupation of head of household.[92]

TABLE II-22: GROUP II (Fall, 1972).

Category Label	n	%
0. No response	57	6.2
1. Prof., Technical	165	18.1
2. Mgr., Official, Prop.	61	6.7
3. Clerical, Sales	51	5.6
4. Crafts, Fore., Mech.	95	10.4
5. Mach. Opr., Driver	88	9.6
6. HH Serv., Mil., Police	114	12.5
7. Laborer, Teamster	153	16.7
8. Farm Mgr., Worker	56	6.1
9. Not in work force	74	8.1
TOTAL	914	100.0

TABLE III-22: GROUP III (Spring, 1973).

Category Label	n	%
0. No response	63	6.4
1. Prof. Technical	187	19.0
2. Mgr., Official, Prop.	47	4.8
3. Clerical, Sales	75	7.7
4. Crafts, Fore., Mech.	115	11.7
5. Mach. Opr., Driver	127	12.9
6. HH Serv., Mil., Police	90	9.1
7. Laborer, Teamster	177	18.0
8. Farm Mgr., Worker	37	3.8
9. Not in work force	65	6.6
TOTAL	984	100.0

Q. 23. Self-employment status, head of household.[93]

TABLE II-23: GROUP II (Fall, 1972).

Category Label	n	%
0. No response	85	9.3
1. Yes	175	19.1
2. No	654	71.6
TOTAL	914	100.0

TABLE III-23: GROUP III (Spring, 1973).

Category Label	n	%
0. No response	87	8.8
1. Yes	161	16.4
2. No.	736	74.8
TOTAL	984	100.0

Q. 24. Primary employment status, head of household.[94]

TABLE II-24: GROUP II (Fall, 1972).

Category Label	n	%
0. No response	16	1.8
1. Employed	703	76.9
2. Unemployed	33	3.6
3. Retired	38	4.2
4. Disabled	23	2.5
5. Housewife	46	5.0
6. Student	37	4.0
7. Other	18	2.0
TOTAL	914	100.0

TABLE III-24: GROUP III (Spring, 1973).

Category Label	n	%
0. No response	34	3.5
1. Employed	732	74.4
2. Unemployed	35	3.6
3. Retired	58	5.9
4. Disabled	16	1.6
5. Housewife	40	4.1
6. Student	55	5.6
7. Other	14	1.4
TOTAL	984	100.0

Q. 25. Veteran status of respondent.[95]

TABLE II-25: GROUP II (Fall, 1972).

Category Label	n	%
0. No response	62	6.8
1. Male, Veteran	81	8.9
2. Male, Non-veteran	323	35.3
3. Female, Husband Vet.	18	2.0
4. Female, Husband not Vet.	41	4.5
5. Single Female	389	42.6
TOTAL	914	100.0

TABLE III-25: GROUP III (Spring, 1972).

Category Label	n	%
0. No response	66	6.7
1. Male, Veteran	103	10.5
2. Male, Non-veteran	296	30.1
3. Female, Husband Vet.	27	2.7
4. Female, Husband not Vet.	44	4.5
5. Single Female	448	45.5
TOTAL	984	100.0

Q. 26. Union tie in respondent's family.[96]

TABLE II-26: GROUP II (Fall, 1972).

Category Label	n	%
0. No response	30	3.3
1. None in family	509	55.7
2. R. is member	30	3.3
3. Spouse is member	9	1.0
4. Child is member	1	0.1
5. Sibling is member	94	10.3
6. Parent is member	227	24.8
7. Other member	14	1.5
TOTAL	914	100.0

TOTAL III-26: GROUP III (Spring, 1973).

Category Label	n	%
0. No response	33	3.4
1. None in family	547	55.6
2. R. is member	51	5.2
3. Spouse is member	27	2.7
4. Child is member	0	0.0
5. Sibling is member	84	8.5
6. Parent is member	221	22.5
7. Other member	21	2.1
TOTAL	984	100.0

Q. 27. Religious preference of respondent.[97]

TABLE II-27: GROUP II (Fall, 1972).

Category Label	n	%
0. No response	10	1.1
1. Protestant	693	75.8
2. Catholic	64	7.0
3. Jewish	5	0.5
4. Other	92	10.1
5. No organized church	27	3.0
6. Agnostic	15	1.6
7. Atheist	8	0.9
TOTAL	914	100.0

TABLE III-27: GROUP III (Spring, 1973).

Category Label	n	%
0. No response	19	1.9
1. Protestant	681	69.2
2. Catholic	69	7.0
3. Jewish	4	0.4
4. Other	143	14.5
5. No organized church	38	3.9
6. Agnostic	22	2.2
7. Atheist	8	0.8
TOTAL	984	100.0

Q. 28. Frequency of church attendance.[98]

TABLE II-28: GROUP II (Fall, 1972).

Category Label	n	%
0. No response	12	1.3
1. Regular	308	33.7
2. Often	269	29.4
3. Seldom	289	31.6
4. Never	36	3.9
TOTAL	914	100.0

Mean	2.032	Std. err.	0.031
Mode	1.000	Std. dev.	0.929
Kurtosis	-1.019	Skewness	0.134
Median	2.009	Variance	0.863

Range for computation of statistics: 1 through 4.

TABLE III-28: GROUP III (Spring, 1973).

Category Label	n	%
0. No response	10	1.0
1. Regular	323	32.8
2. Often	260	26.4
3. Seldom	336	34.1
4. Never	55	5.6
TOTAL	984	100.0

Mean	2.105	Std. err.	0.031
Mode	3.000	Std. dev.	0.961
Kurtosis	-1.090	Skewness	0.099
Median	2.112	Variance	0.924

Range for computation of statistics: 1 through 4.

Q. 29.   Perception of family social class.[99]

TABLE II-29:   GROUP II (Fall, 1972).

Category Label	n	%
0. No response	7	0.8
1. Lower/working	268	29.3
2. Lower-middle	208	22.8
3. Middle-middle	338	37.0
4. Upper-middle	79	8.6
5. Upper class	14	1.5
TOTAL	914	100.0

Mean	2.280	Std. err.	0.035
Mode	3.000	Std. dev.	1.049
Kurtosis	-0.775	Skewness	0.152
Median	2.375	Variance	1.100

Range for computation of statistics: 1 through 5.

TABLE III-29:   GROUP III (Spring, 1973).

Category Label	n	%
0. No response	17	1.7
1. Lower/working	295	30.0
2. Lower-middle	255	25.9
3. Middle-middle	333	33.8
4. Upper-middle	72	7.3
5. Upper class	12	1.2
TOTAL	984	100.0

Mean	2.187	Std. err.	0.033
Mode	3.000	Std. dev.	1.037
Kurtosis	-0.671	Skewness	0.184
Median	2.206	Variance	1.076

Range for computation of statistics: 1 through 5.

Q. 30. Sex of respondent.[100]

TABLE II-30: GROUP II (Fall, 1972).

Category Label	n	%
0. No response	20	2.2
1. Female	480	52.5
2. Male	414	45.3
TOTAL	914	100.0

TABLE III-30: GROUP III (Spring, 1973).

Category Label	n	%
0. No response	25	2.5
1. Female	554	56.3
2. Male	405	41.2
TOTAL	984	100.0

Q. 32. Home ownership by head of household.[101]

TABLE II-32: GROUP II (Fall, 1972).

Category Label	n	%
0. No response	68	7.4
1. Own home	615	67.3
2. Rent home	175	19.1
3. Other	56	6.1
TOTAL	914	100.0

TABLE III-32: GROUP III (Spring, 1973).

Category Label	n	%
0. No response	48	4.9
1. Own home	610	62.0
2. Rent home	270	27.4
3. Other ·	56	5.7
TOTAL	984	100.0

Q. 33. Perception of income (not recoded).[102]

TABLE II-33: GROUP II (Fall, 1972).

Category Label	n	%
00. No response	79	8.6
01. Under $1,000	41	4.5
02. $ 1,000-$ 1,999	60	6.6
03. $ 2,000-$ 2,999	75	8.2
04. $ 3,000-$ 3,999	93	10.2
05. $ 4,000-$ 4,999	71	7.8
06. $ 5,000-$ 5,999	71	7.8
07. $ 6,000-$ 6,999	57	6.2
08. $ 7,000-$ 7,999	62	6.8
09. $ 8,000-$ 8,999	60	6.6
10. $ 9,000-$ 9,999	43	4.7
11. $10,000-$11,999	65	7.1
12. $12,000-$14,999	50	5.5
13. $15,000-$19,999	40	4.4
14. $20,000-$24,999	20	2.2
15. $25,000-$49,999	22	2.4
16. $50,000 and over	5	0.5
TOTAL	914	100.0

Mean	6.487	Std. err.	0.139
Mode	4.000	Std. dev.	4.214
Kurtosis	-0.947	Skewness	0.237
Median	6.035	Variance	17.755

Range for computation of statistics: 1 through 16.

Q. 33.   Perception of income (not   recoded).[102]

TABLE III-33: GROUP III (Spring, 1973).

Category Label	n	%
00. No response	76	7.7
01. Under $1,000	24	2.4
02. $ 1,000-$ 1,999	39	4.0
03. $ 2,000-$ 2,999	52	5.3
04. $ 3,000-$ 3,999	84	8.5
05. $ 4,000-$ 4,999	58	5.9
06. $ 5,000-$ 5,999	61	6.2
07. $ 6,000-$ 6,999	73	7.4
08. $ 7,000-$ 7,999	86	8.7
09. $ 8,000-$ 8,999	65	6.6
10. $ 9,000-$ 9,999	64	6.5
11. $10,000-$11,999	80	8.1
12. $12,000-$14,999	82	8.3
13. $15,000-$19,999	70	7.1
14. $20,000-$24,999	38	3.9
15. $25,000-$49,999	25	2.5
16. $50,000 and over	7	0.7
TOTAL	984	100.0

Mean	7.588	Std. err.	0.136
Mode	8.000	Std. dev.	4.268
Kurtosis	-0.994	Skewness	-0.135
Median	7.791	Variance	18.214

Range for computation of statistics: 1 through 16.

Q. 33.   Perception of income (recoded).[102]

TABLE II-33:   GROUP II (Fall, 1972).

Category Label	n	%
0. No response	79	8.6
1. $ 0-$ 2,999	176	19.3
2. $ 3,000-$ 6,999	292	31.9
3. $ 7,000-$ 9,999	165	18.1
4. $10,000-$14,999	115	12.6
5. $15,000-$24,999	60	6.6
6. $25,000-$49,999	22	2.4
7. $50,000 and over	5	0.5
TOTAL	914	100.0

Mean	2.387	Std. err.	0.049
Mode	2.000	Std. dev.	1.479
Kurtosis	-0.062	Skewness	0.527
Median	2.192	Variance	2.187

Range for computation of statistics: 1 through 7.

TABLE III-33:   GROUP III (Spring, 1973).

Category Label	n	%
0. No response	76	7.7
1. $ 0-$ 2,999	115	11.7
2. $ 3,000-$ 6,999	276	28.0
3. $ 7,000-$ 9,999	215	21.8
4. $10,000-$14,999	162	16.5
5. $15,000-$24,999	108	11.0
6. $25,000-$49,999	25	2.5
7. $50,000 and over	7	0.7
TOTAL	984	100.0

Mean	2.743	Std. err.	0.049
Mode	2.000	Std. dev.	1.525
Kurtosis	-0.410	Skewness	0.195
Median	2.616	Variance	2.325

Range for compuatation of statistics: 1 through 7.

Q. 34.   Perception of Nixon as a real Republican.[103]

TABLE II-34:   GROUP II (Fall, 1972).

Category Label	n	%
0. No response	44	4.8
1. Yes	542	59.3
2. No	328	35.9
TOTAL	914	100.0

TABLE III-34:   GROUP III (Spring, 1973).

Category Label	n	%
0. No response	52	5.3
1. Yes	620	63.0
2. No	312	31.7
TOTAL	984	100.0

Q. 35.   Perception of Johnson as a real Democrat.[104]

TABLE II-35:   GROUP II (Fall, 1972).

Category Label	n	%
0. No response	44	4.8
1. Yes	567	62.0
2. No	303	33.2
TOTAL	914	100.0

TABLE III-35: GROUP III (Spring, 1973).

Category Label	n	%
0. No response	54	5.5
1. Yes	704	71.5
2. No	226	23.0
TOTAL	984	100.0